# PICTORIAL HISTORY OF

# FREDERICK

## MARYLAND

D1104439

## The First 250 Years
## 1745-1995

TIMOTHY L. CANNON • TOM GORSLINE • NANCY F. WHITMORE

Copyright © 1995 by Timothy L. Cannon, Thomas C. Gorsline, and Nancy F. Whitmore.

Library of Congress Catalog Card Number 95-075892

ISBN 0-9645300-0-7 (Leather); 0-9645300-1-5 (Hard cover); 0-9645300-2-3 (Paperback)

For information, write:
Key Publishing Group
6 East Street, Suite 301
Frederick, Maryland 21701

Printed in the United States of America
M&B Printing, Frederick, Maryland

This project was made possible in part by support from Farmers and Mechanics National Bank, Frederick County National Bank, Fredericktown Bank, M&B Printing, and State Farm Insurance.

# CONTENTS

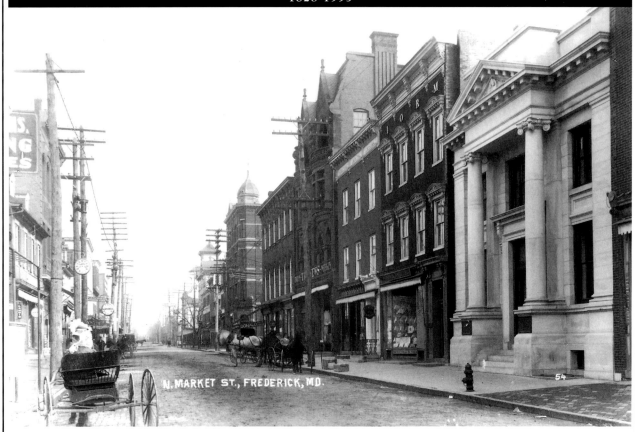

# PREFACE

In celebration of Frederick City's 250th anniversary, the publishers are proud to offer this pictorial history chronicling two-and-one-half centuries of life in our home. Tim Cannon and Nancy Whitmore, who published a similar work 14 years ago, joined forces with *Frederick Magazine* Publisher Tom Gorsline to produce this new work, *A Pictorial History of Frederick—The First 250 Years.*

We have made every effort to achieve high quality in copying and reproducing the photographs and negatives acquired for this book. Many of our photographs have come from original sources, such as glass-plate negatives. The photos were reproduced using a computer digitizing process that achieves a much higher quality reproduction than simply taking a photograph of a photograph.

By profession, we are not historians, but we have made every effort to assure the accuracy of the written material used in the text and captions. We gathered together a group of individuals well-versed in Frederick's history to assist us. They graciously spent many hours reviewing some of the written material. We thank them for their diligence and time: Harry Decker, Carroll Hendrickson, Richard Lebherz, and Theresa Mathias Michel.

As with all such endeavors, there are many people who have made this book possible. We thank Richard Markey, James Ochs, and Brian James of OakLeaf Communications for their design assistance. We also wish to thank Susan Holly and Julie Summers Walker for their editorial input. Special thanks to Edna Jean Lauch and Ann Miller for their assistance with advance book sales.

Finally, and most importantly, this book would not be possible without the generosity of those who shared their fine collections of photographs and negatives with us: C. Burr Artz Library, Carl Brown, Bob Gearinger of Fredericktown Bank, Paul and Rita Gordon, the Historical Society of Frederick County, Patsy Moore, Stanley Sundergill, Karl Zimmerman, and the many area citizens who responded so generously to our request for pictures. We are especially grateful to Carl Brown for his comprehensive photo history that spans almost six decades. He is to be praised for capturing on film so many of the buildings that have been razed in the name of progress.

Now it is time to relax, put your feet up, and enjoy our past.

*Tim Cannon, Tom Gorsline, Nancy Whitmore*

# FOREWORD

As mayor of the City of Frederick, I invite you to step into this *Pictorial History of Frederick—The First 250 Years*, and be a guest through two-and-one-half centuries of charm, culture, architecture, and flavor of one of the most vibrant communities in the United States.

Frederick, founded in 1745 by English and German settlers., is an historic city distinguished by Colonial and Federal architecture in the heart of Maryland. Visits by presidents Washington and Lincoln, the Marquis de LaFayette, and statesman Benjamin Franklin have laid the groundwork for our rich history. Frederick has not only survived the Revolutionary and Civil War eras and two World Wars, but it has thrived.

Frederick City now boasts more than 45,000 residents, but we are really a small town at heart. As a native Frederick County resident, I have witnessed many changes in Frederick, but can attest that one thing has never changed: small-town friendliness smiles at you from every street corner.

Witness our annual events: the "In the Street" festival allows our businesses to swing wide their doors, welcoming customers strolling the streets of our historic city; the Frederick Festival of the Arts and craft fairs held at Creekside welcome visitors with open arms to celebrate our downtown beauty; the Holidays in Historic Frederick are nothing short of magical as the city glows with candle-light and offers a wealth of wonderful activities. Year-round, the Weinberg and Delaplaine centers offer performing and visual arts that please the most discriminating tastes.

Frederick's own professional baseball stadium, golf course, swimming pools, and play areas located throughout the city demonstrate the area's emphasis on family activities.

While our small-town face has not changed, our business climate has. Our area has grown from an agricultural community in the 1700s to today's vibrant business community. Some of the largest and most successful companies in the country that offer employment to our very diverse and educated population have settled in the area, and our proximity to metropolitan centers and multi-transportation systems make Frederick a sought-after site for new business.

As we celebrate in 1995 the 250th anniversary of the 1745 founding of Frederick, let us be thankful that our forefathers created this warm and vibrant community and left to us the legacy of liberty observed in this book.

The *Pictorial History of Frederick-The First 250 Years* walks you through the changes over the last 250 years and brings you up to the future. You can see the direction the future will take as you stroll through Frederick's past.

Welcome to the future!

James S. Grimes
Mayor
City of Frederick

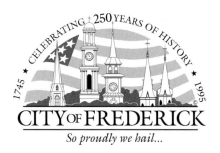

CITY OF FREDERICK
*So proudly we hail...*

# ERICK COUNTY BANK

## 1818-1995

# Frederick's Center of Business and Community

The year was 1818, and the county known as Frederick was flourishing as it ranked the second largest agricultural community in the United States. Times were good. And a new bank was born, the oldest bank founded and headquartered in Frederick County, FCNB Bank, then known as the Frederick County Bank.

One North Market Street was the Bank's original site, a most prominent location that would grow to be the business center of Frederick. FCNB Bank's founders numbered among them the most notable men of their time. Enterprising and keen, they seized the moment.

The first president was John Colin Grahame, son-

in-law to Maryland's first governor, Thomas Johnson. First directors included statesman, Roger Brooke Taney. With them, George Baer, first cashier, William Goldsborough, John Christian Kemp, Frederick A. Schley, Abraham Shriver, Henry Steiner, and John P. Thomson contributed their

wisdom and foresight to mold the framework of the Bank. They chartered the Bank to strongly serve the community, to grow in service and product offerings as customers and Frederick prospered. How visionary and sound in their plans they were.

From a still unresolved robbery in 1841, to Confederate Jubal Early's ransom, to the Great Depression's bust, to post-World War II boom times, FCNB Bank has always been here, a full service financial institution meeting the personal and

business needs of all customers. FCNB Bank, the long-standing nickname, became official on June 1, 1993.

From its beginnings and all along the way, FCNB Bank has kept in step with the times, bringing progress to banking while keeping the traditions that serve the community well.

*FCNB Bank, Frederick's Center of Business and Community*

# FCNB
### ▋▋▋BANK

Member FDIC
1 North Market Street
Frederick, Maryland

# DANIEL DULANY

Daniel Dulany, the elder, founder of Frederick, came to Maryland as an indentured servant in 1703. At the time of his death 50 years later, he was one of the wealthiest and most influential men in the colony. He was born in Queens County, Ireland, in 1685 to a family with few resources. With the meager funds his father could provide, Dulany studied for a time at the University of Dublin before deciding to seek his fortune in the New World.

Dulany arrived in Port Tobacco, Maryland, at the age of 18 along with his two older brothers, William and Joseph. He was spared the usual indentured servitude by a colonial, George Plater, who paid for his passage and put him to work in his law office to help with plantation accounts. Plater needed law clerks, and Dulany was someone with obvious intelligence and university training. From this beginning, Dulany became a practicing lawyer, judge, member of the Maryland Assembly, attorney general for the colony, planter and land speculator.

As a member of the Maryland Assembly from Annapolis in 1728, Dulany wrote a pamphlet entitled "The Right of the Inhabitants of Maryland to the Benefit of English Laws." This powerful pamphlet expressed his party's views, contested by Lord Baltimore, that colonists had the same rights as Englishmen. This was one of the earliest expressions of a theme that would reappear at the time of the revolution. Dulany, however, would later change sides in this debate, after Lord Baltimore offered him positions in the colonial establishment.

Dulany began buying land in western Maryland in the 1720s. By the 1740s, he owned five large tracts of land in what is now Frederick County. He was joined by Benjamin Tasker, who was developing a large parcel near the Monocacy River called Tasker's Chance. The land was considered to be the most fertile in the area. Dulany laid out the streets of Frederick on the eastern side of Tasker's Chance in September 1745. He speculated that he could develop a strong center of trade here that could market and trade goods with England.

Dulany was married three times. His first wife, Charity Courts Smallwood, was the daughter and widow of wealthy planters. She died in 1711 after only a year of marriage, and her land reverted to her family. Two years later Dulany remarried, again to a planter's daughter, named Rebecca Smith. In 1722, she bore him a son, Daniel Dulany, the younger, who would become as prominent as his father. Rebecca died in 1737. After a year, Dulany married Henrietta Lloyd Chew, a young widow with six children and a plentiful fortune.

Dulany died in Annapolis, Maryland, on December 5, 1753. He was survived by Henrietta and numerous children.

HISTORY OF FREDERICK 1745-1995

Thomas Johnson

# CHAPTER 1

## 1745-1799

Frederick Founded by Daniel Dulany in 1745

Schifferstadt Completed

Washington, Franklin and Braddock Confer Here
During French and Indian War

Hessian Barracks Built

Thomas Johnson Moves to Frederick

Old Town Mill Built

Frederick, or Fredericktown as it was then called, was founded in September 1745 by a successful land speculator named Daniel Dulany, the Elder. He laid out the town on the eastern edge of a tract of land known as Tasker's Chance—some 7,000 acres along both sides of Carroll Creek from its mouth on the Monocacy River west to approximately where U. S. Route 15 is today.

Fredericktown was probably named after Frederick Calvert, sixth and last Lord Baltimore; but there is speculation it may have been named in honor of Frederick Lewis, Prince of Wales, son of George II and father of George III.

The back country that was then western Maryland, where Frederick was located, had been settled rather quickly. What was mostly woods in 1730 had become Frederick County in 1748. By 1755 it was the most populated county in Maryland. Fredericktown, the county seat, was the most populated city in the county.

The great land movement to Maryland's western lands was probably started by Lord Baltimore's very liberal land offer in March 1732. This was an attempt to attract German immigrant farmers, who by then had become dissatisfied with many of the other provinces.

*Courtesy of Paul and Rita Gordon*

*Artist's conception of the first house in the original Fredericktown, located on the northeast corner of East Patrick Street and Middle Alley. Built in 1746 by John Thomas Schley, a schoolteacher, this house stood until 1853.*

*Frederick Calvert, the sixth and last Lord Baltimore, is the probable namesake of the city of Frederick.*

*Courtesy of Anonymous Donor*

Another offer, around the same time, of fertile lands in the Shenandoah Valley of Virginia by the royal governor of that colony, also brought Germans from Pennsylvania—going south—into the Frederick area. With the influx of farmers, the back country needed a trading center and shipping point, and Fredericktown satisfied these requirements.

Dulany laid out the streets of Frederick in straight lines running north-south and east-west. The sole exception was the bend that occurs in West Patrick Street, which was probably made to avoid marshy ground. The original lots, laid out on both sides of Carroll Creek, were 60 feet and 63 feet wide and 355 feet to 393 feet deep. By 1781, 200 of these lots were sold.

In 1755, Fredericktown already had 200 houses and three churches, one English and two German. The English, too, including many from the Tidewater, had been coming into the area from the south, following the Potomac River into the southern part of the county. They owned most of the land and held positions in government. Nonetheless, it would be many years before English could be heard more often than German on Frederick's streets.

Probably the most important event to affect the lives of the early Fredericktonians was the French and Indian War.

*Courtesy of Anonymous Donor*

*Courtesy of City of Frederick*

*The first courthouse was located on Council Street and was built on three acres that Daniel Dulany sold for the construction of a building "to the use of the inhabitants of the said County to build a Court House and prison thereon and to no other use, intent, or purpose whatsoever." The wood-frame exterior was completed on November 24, 1750; however, the interior was not finished until 1756.*

*This building was the site of the repudiation of the Stamp Act in 1765 and the execution of three Tory supporters (including Casper Fritchie, the father-in-law of Barbara Fritchie) on August 17, 1781. The extreme sentence handed down by Judge Alexander Contree Hanson was that they be "hanged and cut down to earth alive, and your entrails shall be taken out and burnt while you are alive, and your heads shall be cut off, your body shall be divided into four parts and be placed where his excellency the Governor shall appoint." The sentence was later reduced to death by hanging.*

*Courtesy of Meredith Springer*

# SCHIFFERSTADT

Schifferstadt, completed in 1756, is the oldest standing building in Frederick. Located on the corner of Second Street and Rosemont Avenue next to Route 15, it is a fine example of German colonial architecture with its 2½-foot-thick walls, hand-hewn oak beams, large vaulted chimney, paling insulated interior walls, exposed half-timbering, and "cross and bible" doors with highly wrought elbow locks and hinges. On the second floor can be found a five-plate, or jamb, stove, one of the three used to heat the house, with a German inscription: "Where your treasure is, there is your heart." The stove, cast in

*Authors' Collection*

1756 at Elizabeth Furnace in Lancaster County, Pennsylvania, is believed to be the inspiration for the Franklin stove.

The farm property was named for Kleinschifferstadt, Germany, the birthplace of the original owner, Joseph Brunner. Records indicate that Joseph Prundar had been released from serfdom on April 26, 1729. He signed his name as Joseph Brunner when he and his family arrived aboard the *Allen* at the port of Philadelphia on September 11, 1729. The Brunners' settled briefly near Lancaster. Lured by Lord Baltimore's offer of cheap land, the Brunners joined many other German immigrants who traveled to western Maryland and founded the Monocacy settlement. For the sum of one cent per acre per year after the fourth year, the settlers were able to obtain 200 acres of farm land on Maryland's western boundary. This generous offer was made

not only to lure the industrious German settlers from Pennsylvania but also to provide a buffer between the Indians, who were being forced farther and farther westward, and the established coastal settlements. On July 28, 1746, a deed was granted to Joseph Brunner for 303 acres of the 7,000-acre tract of land called Tasker's Chance. The cost was ten English pounds. Joseph Brunner called his farm "Scheverstadt."

There is no record of the first buildings erected on the property between 1736 and 1746, but in all likelihood they were temporary and functional log buildings. It was common for the German settlers to build temporary buildings until they could afford a proper residence. There is no record of Joseph Brunner's wife, Catharina, living in Maryland. It is believed that she died prior to the move to the Monocacy settlement.

On January 17, 1753, Joseph deeded Schifferstadt to his youngest son, Elias, for the sum of 200 pounds. This was a common practice among the German immigrants in Pennsylvania and Maryland because the older sons were generally married and established on their own farm nearby. Joseph Brun-

ner probably resided with his son and daughter-in-law, Albertina, until his death.

In 1771, at the age of 48, Elias retired to town and sold the property for 1,500 pounds.

In 1974, Schifferstadt, along with three acres of surrounding land, was purchased by Frederick County Landmarks Foundation, Inc., for $65,000. Today the building serves as a gallery and museum and is open for tours. For the past several years, Landmarks has hosted an Oktoberfest on the grounds.

The illustration on the previous page depicts the interior of Schifferstadt. The house faces the southeast to take advantage of morning sunshine. On the north end of the house is the kitchen, located directly above the cellar. The parlor is located on the south side of the house. Fireplaces vent directly into a centrally located chimney. Bedrooms, with the exception of the master bedroom, are located on the second floor. Shake shingles cover the high pitched roof, allowing for a spacious attic.

In 1755 General Edward Braddock arrived from England with 1,400 troops to fight the French and Indians in North America. Braddock stopped in Frederick during the spring of that year on his way to attack the French at Fort Duquesne, the present site of Pittsburgh. Colonial forces had been added, including a young colonel named George Washington, who met Braddock in Frederick.

Benjamin Franklin also came to Frederick at this time. Franklin, who was an influential man in Pennsylvania, helped Braddock procure the wagons needed for the trip. This was necessary because only about 25 wagons, along with every available horse, could be commandeered from the Frederick area, prompting the general to describe it as "this dreary and desolate place."

Food supplies, however, were plentiful, and area

*Authors' Collection*

*A photograph of "Washington's Headquarters," located on the south bank of Carroll Creek, south of the Hanson house. The building, believed to have been a tavern, was torn down in the 1960s. Colonel George Washington was said to have used this structure on April 30, 1755, during the French and Indian War, on joining General Edward Braddock as an aide-de-camp. Also, Franklin, Washington, and Braddock may have used this building to make plans for the ill-fated mission to take Fort Duquesne.*

*General Edward Braddock, commander of British forces in America, stopped in Frederick in April 1755 on his way to defeat and death near Fort Duquesne during the French and Indian War.*

*Courtesy of the Historical Society of Frederick County, Inc.*

farmers were eager to sell Braddock's men such staples as beef, eggs, chicken, lamb, pork, and milk. In late April or early May, Braddock's army, still short of wagons, left Frederick heading west for South Mountain. A small group of Frederick County sharpshooters volunteered to go along, dressed as Indians. The absence from the community of the wagons and drivers that Braddock had commandeered probably delayed the completion of Frederick's first courthouse until 1756.

Braddock suffered a terrible defeat at Fort Duquesne, where he sustained severe wounds that resulted in his death near Fort Necessity. As a result, the Indian tribes that had supported the English now supported the French. Almost every Maryland settler west of South Mountain was killed. Fredericktown must have lived in constant fear that it too would be attacked.

The treaty of Paris, signed in 1763, ended the war, with England the victor. Faced with a huge war debt, England levied a succession of unpopular taxes on the colonies, including the infamous 1765 Stamp Act, requiring almost all legal documents, almanacs, newspapers and their advertisements, as well as dice and playing cards, to be taxed and payment to be made in sterling. It also required that legal docu-

(continued on page 22)

Authors' Collection

# JOHN HANSON

This portrait of John Hanson was painted by John Hesse Lius in 1770. Hanson was born in Calvert County, Maryland, on April 13, 1721. He moved to Frederick in 1773 and lived here until 1783. Hanson was an early supporter for the cause against the British. Before coming to Frederick County, he helped draft instructions to Maryland delegates at the Stamp Act Congress in 1765, and in 1769 he signed Maryland's non-importation agreement, adopted to protest the Townsend Acts. Hanson represented Frederick County in Maryland's General Assembly from 1773 to 1779, when he was elected as a Maryland delegate to the Continental Congress. During the revolution, he was active in raising troops and providing ammunition for the county. He was also selected a member of a committee by the Maryland Convention to establish a flint-lock factory in Frederick. Under his leadership, Frederick County delegates to the Maryland Convention were the first in the state to support independence from Britain. He signed the Articles of Confederation, but like the other Maryland delegates, not until the other states had given up their right to lands in the West. In 1781 Hanson was elected first president of the Congress under the Articles of Confederation, prompting some to say that he was technically the first president of the United States. He retired after a one-year term, dying shortly thereafter at Oxon Hill on November 22, 1783. Hanson was married to Jane Contee, with whom he had nine children.

*Portrait of Thomas Johnson and his wife, Ann Jennings, and their three oldest children, Thomas, Ann, and Rebecca, painted by Charles Wilson Peale in 1772. Currently on loan to the Baltimore Museum of Art, the portrait is owned by the trustees of the C. Burr Artz Library.*

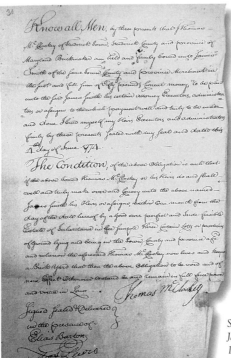

*The building where the Stamp Act was recorded, circa 1908. Built about 1750, this one-story home at 103 Record Street was the home of William Ritchie, clerk of the Frederick County Court from 1779 to 1815. Mr. Ritchie often conducted court business from the porch, leading some to believe it was the actual site of the repudiation of the Stamp Act in 1765. However, there is no proof that the 12 immortal judges signed the document here. The building was demolished in 1910.*

*Statement of Thomas McCloskey of Frederick, binding himself to James Smith, brickmaker, for the sum of 50 pounds, dated 4 June 1774, witnessed by Elias Barton and Thomas Lewis.*

# TRINITY CHAPEL

Trinity Chapel, West Church Street, shown about 1880, was located next to the Independent Fire Company. In the distance is the spire of All Saints Church. The land where the chapel stands was donated to the elders of the Evangelical Reformed Church by the Dulany family in 1746. The first church was erected in 1747. In 1764 a new church was built on the same site.

The tower, the oldest in Maryland, contains some of the original undressed timbers. Lewis Hemp, fourth pastor, was buried beneath the tower in 1807.

The wooden steeple was designed and built by Stephen Steiner. The town clock, built by Frederick Heisly in 1796, was installed upon completion of the steeple, and the weather vane added. In 1880, the

church building, with the exception of the tower, was torn down and rebuilt. It was dedicated as Trinity Chapel on May 21, 1882, for use as a church school. Trinity Chapel is located across West Church Street from the present Evangelical Reformed Church. For many years in the 19th century, the building on the corner was the office of the *Frederick Examiner*.

*Photograph by J. Davis Byerly, Authors' Collection*

Photograph by J. Davis Byerly. Courtesy of Paul and Rita Gordon

# HESSIAN BARRACKS

These colonial barracks, known as the Hessian Barracks, were built by Abraham Faw shortly after the outbreak of the War for Independence. The stone barracks were the result of one of the first acts of the Maryland General Assembly, passed on February 5, 1777, and signed by Governor Thomas Johnson on April 18, 1777. The original purpose was to quarter the American troops stationed in Frederick in the barracks, rather than in private homes. The stone structures would also serve as an arsenal and a place to house prisoners of war, many of them Hessian soldiers.

During the revolution, prisoners were housed in log huts that they built around the barracks. After the war, an armorer was appointed to care for the building and the arsenal. The position of state armorer was abolished in February 1851.

When General Burgoyne's army surrendered in 1779, they were to have been marched to Boston for transport to England. Instead, they were ordered to Virginia. They were finally allowed to travel to New York, but were confined at the barracks from November 1780 until July 1781. While they were held in Frederick, many of the prisoners deserted and a great many died, especially as the result of excessive drinking. Soon after the British prisoners departed, the Hessian soldiers who surrendered at Yorktown arrived at the barracks. These soldiers were not well guarded and many of them deserted and were hired by the German farmers in the surrounding countryside. In September 1781, Congress ordered all deserters to report to Fredericktown, where they were allowed to ransom themselves by paying 80 Spanish dollars — a sum in most cases paid by Fredericktonians.

French sailors captured by the *Constellation* were held at the barracks in 1799, and a fire on June 26, 1799, destroyed the right wing of the barracks.

From 1853 to 1860, the grounds were used to hold the Frederick County Agricultural Society fairs, but they were suspended during the Civil War.

The 1st Maryland Regiment of the Potomac Home Brigade was encamped at the barracks for a time. In August 1861, Brigadier General Nathaniel Banks, a former governor of Massachusetts, established Frederick as the site of a military depot and the Union Military Hospital under the administration of Dr. R. F. Weir. This was one of the largest military hospitals, caring for as many as 900 patients. The doctors were aided by the Ladies' Relief Society organized by Mrs. Gideon Bantz in September 1861.

In 1867, the state took charge of the barracks and in 1868 opened what is now the Maryland School for the Deaf with 34 students. One of the barracks was demolished in 1872-1873 to make way for the school.

*(continued from page 18)*

ments be printed on special paper embossed with a stamp. In August the stamp distributor was burned in effigy by the citizens of Frederick, and on November 1, when the tax went into effect, there were demonstrations in many cities.

In November, the Frederick County court met and defiantly ordered that all business should be transacted without stamps. The officials felt justified in making their decision because the act had not been officially published and they had not received any stamps. The court officially repudiated the Stamp Act on November 23, 1765, and Frederick's action is believed to be the first official repudiation in the colonies.

On November 30, the court's actions were celebrated at a mock funeral. The "body" of the Stamp Act was placed in a coffin and buried, after being displayed in a funeral parade conducted by the town's military company and the Sons of Liberty.

Although the Stamp Act was repealed March 18, 1766, in 1767 the British applied taxes to other items, such as paper, glass, and tea, eventually resulting in the closing of the port of Boston in 1774. On May 20, 1774, at a meeting in the Frederick County courthouse, presided over by John Hanson, Frederick's

*Letter from Abraham Faw in Fredericktowne, builder of the Hessian Barracks, to Governor Thomas Johnson, Annapolis, May 18, 1779.*

*On the far right is an exact transcript of the letter.*

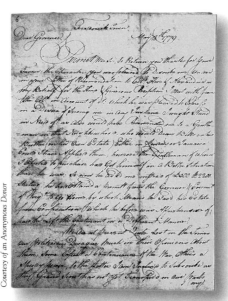

*"Fredericktown, May 18th, 1779*

*Dear Governor,*

*Permit me sire to return you thanks for your favour: the character you was pleased to describe me under in your letter of recommendation to Col. Hood of Alexandria in my behalf for the kind and generous reception I met with from the Colonel on account of it which he was pleased to express in a desire of serving me in any instance I might stand in need of: as also would have recommended me to a gentleman in that neighborhood who would draw bills on his brother (on his own estate) either in London or Jamaica could I have supplied them; however the gentleman of whom I expected to purchase had got himself in a better situation than he was, so now he asked me instead of $500, 2,200 pounds sterling he has obtained a permit from the Governor of Virginia to go home, by which means he saved his estate from confiscation, which he was before apprehensive of had he left the continent in a different manner. We are at present quite lost in the times. Our politicians disagree much in the opinion about them, some expect a continuation of the war, others a speedy peace. So the letter I am enclosing to subscribe as the Grand Scout has not yet transpired in our parts, my conjecture is that some overture of peace has been made by Britain to Congress which I hope will conclude the war by a happy peace.*

*Under the consideration I have had in contemplation the selling my piece of land on Bennetts Creek as I believe I might now get perhaps six times the money for it, that it would sell at shares the credit of the money to better establish here, and the real estate is not so considerable, the greatest part thereof being broken through, the bottom not large enough for a plantation of a necessary estate to support a considerable family. I should under these circumstances esteem your advice Sir, as a singular favor about the matter. The confidence I have of your judgement, candour of extensive correspondence, as also your kind affable and generous disposition is my inducement for troubling you about my little matter which nothing but your good nature could excuse.*

*SIGNED: Abraham Faw*
*I am Sir very respectfully Your obedient Humble servant"*

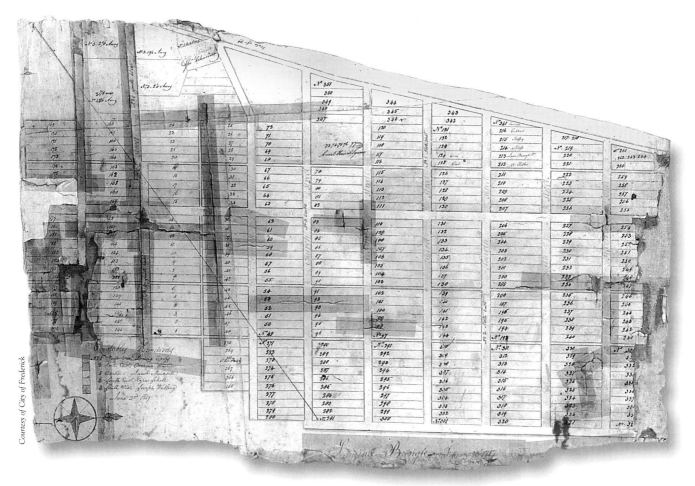

*Courtesy of City of Frederick*

*Authors' Collection*

Frederick City as it appeared in 1787. This map was prepared by Laurence Brengle and is dated February 23, 1787. Mr. Brengle's property is lot number 213 on Fourth Street. In 1817, the citizens of Frederick elected Brengle the first mayor. He resigned in 1818.

The wreckage of the Bantz warehouse, circa 1890, is shown above. The three-story warehouse of stone and brick, located on Brewer's Alley (now Court Street, from Patrick to South streets), was built about 1797 by Dr. William S. Bantz. It was later owned and operated by Gideon Bantz, and was part of the flourishing tanning industry located in the city. In 1853 Bantz and five other tanning firms produced more than 100,000 sides of leather.

Gideon Bantz was more than a successful businessman: he was the first president of the Farmers' Club in 1849; one of the original incorporators of the Franklin Savings Bank; judge of the Orphan's Court from 1843 to 1847; and a member of the House of Delegates in a 1847.

Mrs. Bantz was also civic-minded. In August 1861 she helped found, and was president of, the Ladies' Relief Society, an organization that provided vital assistance to the medical staff of the federal forces, especially after the battles of South Mountain, Antietam, Gettysburg, and Monocacy.

citizens strongly opposed the closing of the port of Boston and were in favor of cutting off all trade with the British.

In December, Frederick citizens decided to form a company of militia, composed of all able-bodied men between the ages of 16 and 50. No important military action took place in or near Frederick County during the revolution, but many Frederick men fought. Maryland troops, in general, were among the best in the Continental Army and saved the day in many a battle.

In late 1778, a prisoner marching through Frederick on his way to Charlottesville, Virginia, described the town as follows: "Fredericktown is a fine large town and has a very noble appearance as the houses are mostly brick and stone, there being very few timbered buildings in it; it contains nearly 2,000 inhabitants, chiefly Ger-mans, quite inland, the nearest port being George-town, which is 50 miles distant, the only river which is the Potowmack [sic] is eight miles from the town..."

The Hessian Barracks, completed in 1778, were used to house British and German prisoners captured at Saratoga, Trenton, and Yorktown. The barracks were described as comfort-able and the prisoners were well supplied. They were allowed to travel

*Clayton Thomas of Frederick County gave the oath of allegiance and fidelity to the State of Maryland, dated 26 February 1778, and signed by Jacob Young, justice of the peace. This oath was taken often during the revolution, usually by people of suspect loyalties.*

*Courtesy of an Anonymous Donor*

STATE OF MARYLAND; *Frederick-County*, viz:

I DO hereby certify, that *Christian Thomas* of said county, hath personally appeared before me the subscriber, one of the justices of the peace for the county aforesaid; and voluntarily taken and subscribed the *oath* of *allegiance*, and *fidelity*; as directed by an act of general assembly of this state; passed the day of *December* A. D. 1777. Witness my hand, and seal, the 26 day of *February* 1778. *Jacob Young* [Sea]

FREDERICK-TOWN: *Printed by* MATTHIAS BARTGIS.

*Courtesy of an Anonymous Donor*

*Proclamation of the appointment of Thomas Johnson of Frederick, Maryland, to the Supreme Court of the United States as an associate justice, on 5 August 1791. At the bottom are the signatures of both President George Washington and Thomas Jefferson. To the left is affixed the Seal of the United States.*

about and to buy fresh produce, and some were permitted to hire themselves out for the day to local farmers. The Hessians were especially pleased to be here because many residents spoke German.

In November 1779, a group of Tories planned to rescue British prisoners being held in several locations in Maryland and Virginia. Unfortunately for them, their plans were discovered when an American officer was mistakenly given papers by a Tory courier. Seven of the conspirators were arrested and brought to Frederick, where they were tried by a special court conducted by Alexander Contee Hanson, Colonel James Johnson, and Upton Sheradine. All were found guilty of treason and sentenced to be hung, drawn, and quartered. Executions were carried out against only three of the traitors; the others were pardoned on the condition they return to England and remain there until the war ended.

When word was received in Frederick that the war had ended in March 1783, there was a great celebration with a fireworks display prepared by one of the German officers. The town held a ball to celebrate the arrival of peace, and a German band provided the music. Many of the Hessians decided to remain in Frederick, some buying land

# THOMAS JOHNSON

Thomas Johnson was born in Calvert County, Maryland, November 4, 1732. He studied law under Stephen Bordley and practiced law in Annapolis.

*Courtesy of Maryland Historical Society*

He married an Annapolis woman named Ann Jennings, and they had twelve children.

In 1762 he entered Maryland's Provincial Assembly as a delegate from Anne Arundel County. While there, Johnson helped lead the opposition to the Stamp Act in 1765. In 1774, as a member of the Maryland Convention, Johnson was chosen to be a member of the 1st Continental Congress in Philadelphia. During the 2nd Continental Congress on June 15, 1775, he nominated his friend, George Washington, to become Commander-in-Chief of the Continental Army.

Johnson is believed to have moved to Frederick between 1775 and 1778. He was not in Philadelphia for the signing of the Declaration of Independence, but he voted in Annapolis on July 6, 1776, as the Delegate of Maryland, for the Declaration separating Maryland from England. He was also a member of the convention in 1775 that adopted Maryland's constitution.

Meanwhile, Johnson was nominated 1st Brigadier General of Maryland's militia. He went to Frederick to raise supplies and men before leading 1,800 men to reinforce George Washington in New Jersey in early 1777. While in New Jersey he accepted the position of first governor of Maryland and was re-elected for two more one-year terms, his final term ending November 12, 1779. In 1780 and 1781 Johnson supported the adoption of the Articles of Confederation, but only after the other colonies gave up their rights to the lands west of the Alleghenies.

He was appointed associate justice of the Supreme Court in 1791 but resigned in 1793 because of failing health. In 1795 Washington offered Johnson the position of secretary of state, which he declined due again to his health. Johnson spent his retirement years in Frederick, making his last public appearance in Frederick in 1800 in honor of his good friend, the late George Washington. Johnson died October 6, 1819, at Rose Hill in Frederick and is buried at Mount Olivet Cemetery.

and marrying local women.

In October 1780 the state legislature passed an act to confiscate all British property owned by British subjects in Maryland. Any-one who had left the state was considered a British subject unless he returned by March 1782 and took the oath of allegiance. Because of this act, Daniel Dulany, the Younger, lost his extensive land holdings in Frederick County, including many lots that still belonged to him in Frederick.

In the 1780s sanitary conditions in Frederick, like most towns of the times, were deplorable. The streets were badly graded and unpaved, and there was little drainage. Dry weather produced blinding dust, and wet weather produced deep quagmires of mud. Dead animals often rotted in the streets; the town had no provision for regular garbage removal. There was little in the way of street lighting once public and private dwellings had dashed their lights, usually around nine o'clock.

In 1786 a commission was created to deal with these civic problems. The commission had the power to collect taxes within cer-tain limits for road improvements and could require that property own-ers put footpaths in front of their property. Progress was slow, however. Taxes were kept low because people were unaccustomed

*Letter from President George Washington to Thomas Johnson in Fredericktown, dated 26 August 1795. This letter was written as a result of the delay of a prior letter from Washington to Johnson, dated 24 August 1795. President Washington wished Johnson to respond to the position offered in the letter of the 24th by express, as he remained in Philadelphia only to receive Johnson's answer before going to see his family in Virginia. The position offered Thomas Johnson in the letter was secretary of state.*

*The first part of the August 24 letter reads as follows:*

*"My dear sir:*

*The office of secretary of state is vacant; occasioned by the resignation of Mr. Randolph. Will you accept it? You know my wishes of old, to bring you into the administration; where then is the necessity of repeating them? No time more than the present ever required the aid of your abilities nor of the old and proved patriots of the country. To have yours would be pleasing to me, and I verily believe we'd be agreeable also to the community at large. It is with you to decide . . ."*

*Johnson declined the president's offer because of ill health.*

# ROSE HILL MANOR

Thomas Johnson purchased the 225-acre tract known as Rose Hill in February 1776, as a gift to his eldest daughter, Ann, at the time of her marriage. Her husband, Major John Colin Grahame, built Rose Hill Manor in the 1790s. When Ann Jennings Johnson died in 1794, Ann Grahame invited her father to live at Rose Hill. Thomas Johnson died October 6, 1819, at Rose Hill Manor. Operated by the Frederick County Parks and Recreation Commission in cooperation with the Children's Museum, the Farm Museum, and the Carriage Society, Rose Hill Manor stands today as a symbol of rural colonial architecture and the abundant historical heritage of Frederick. Rose Hill Manor Park and Children's Museum is located on 43 acres and provides visitors with the opportunity to view and participate in colonial life. Costumed volunteers guide visitors through the home and over the grounds, providing information about colonial life. Visitors are shown the ice house, blacksmith shop, carriage museum, farm museum, and an 18th-century garden and orchard.

to paying high taxes.

In the early 1790s President George Washington paid a visit to Fredericktown, staying at the home of his friend, Thomas Johnson. During his short stay Washington graciously and humbly accepted the tribute its citizens willingly bestowed. Before leaving Frederick County for Philadelphia, he spoke these words to a number of area residents:

"My Countrymen, I am about to leave your good land, your beautiful valleys, your refreshing streams and the blue hills of Maryland which stretch out before me. I cannot leave you, fellow citizens, without thanking you again and again for your kind greeting, for the true and devoted friendship you have shown me. When in the darkest hours of the Revolution, of doubt and gloom, the succor and support I received from the people of Frederick County always cheered me. It always awoke a responsive echo in my breast. I feel the emotion of gratitude beating in my heart—my heart is too full to say more— God bless you all." ☆

*Photograph by J. Davis Byerly Authors' Collection*

*The Old Town Mill was probably erected by Jacob Bentz in the late 1700s. The date painted on the front face of the structure was 1787, though some historians think it may have been much older. It was one of the first flour mills in Frederick County and the first structure on what is now Bentz Street. The millrace from Carroll Creek provided the power.*

*Bentz acquired the property from the sale of the confiscated holdings of Daniel Dulany during the revolution.*

*The property was purchased by the Ramsburg family in 1798 and remained in their possession until 1836. Lewis Brunner bought the property in 1848 and operated the mill for 40 years. In 1895 Newton Zentz acquired the property and the mill was known from then on as the Zentz Mill.*

*The mill, which stood on the site of the playground beside the old armory, burned down in 1928, clearing the way for the development of Baker Park.*

# PROSPECT HALL

Prospect Hall, shown here amidst a snowy landscape, dates to the period between 1790 and 1810, with additions and renovations occurring into the 1900s.

The land upon which Prospect Hall stands was originally known as Dickson's Struggle, after James Dickson, who patented the property in 1748. Daniel Dulany, the Younger, after his marriage to Benjamin Tasker's daughter, Rebecca, was given the property by his father in 1749. Colonel John McPherson, Sr., purchased parts of the original property, along with other land, between 1797 and 1829 and is the likely candidate to have built the home. Upon McPherson's death in 1829, the property passed into the hands of his son, William. When William decided to move his family to Frederick, Prospect Hall was used as a boarding school operated by Jonathan Woodbridge from 1830 to 1832.

During the Civil War the mansion had an interesting history. It was owned by Colonel William P. Maulsby, a commanding officer in the Potomac Home Brigade. Around this time, Democratic presidential candidate Stephen Douglas visited here. In 1862, Confederate troops camped on the grounds of Prospect Hall. Before the Battle of Gettysburg in 1863, General Joseph Hooker was relieved of his command by General George G. Meade near Prospect Hall. During the Battle of the Monocacy in 1864, Prospect Hall served as a hospital for sick and wounded Confederate soldiers.

There were eight owners between the end of the Civil War and 1927, including William and Antoinette Denegre, who owned the property for 20 years. Joseph Himes, a congressman from Ohio, owned Prospect Hall from 1927 to 1957. During this time, many notable people visited the estate, including Harry Truman and William O. Douglas. Saint John's Church purchased Prospect Hall in 1957 for use as a high school. In 1972, the Sisters of Notre Dame, who operated the institution, announced they would be leaving the high school, and it was feared that the school would be closed. A group of concerned citizens, led by local attorney James McSherry, were determined to keep the school open. Thus, Saint John's became Prospect Hall, an interdenominational school.

Prospect Hall has been officially recognized by the Maryland Historic Trust, enabling the school to apply for state funds for restoration.

Francis Scott Key

# CHAPTER 2

# 1800-1859

Old Stone Tavern Built

Francis Scott Key Writes Star Spangled Banner

General Lafayette Visits Frederick

B&O Railroad Depot Established

Frederick County National Bank Robbed of $185,000

Winchester Hall Completed

# FRANCIS SCOTT KEY

Francis Scott Key was born to Ann Charlton and John Key at Terra Rubra, a large estate in then Frederick, but now Carroll County, on August 1, 1779. Educated at St. John's College, Annapolis, he studied law in the office of his uncle, Phillip Barton Key, and practiced law in Frederick from 1801 to 1805.

In 1814, during the British withdrawal from Washington, Key's friend Dr. William Beanes of Upper Marlboro was arrested by the British. Key received permission from President James Madison to attempt to secure Dr. Beanes' release. Under a flag of truce, Francis Scott Key, accompanied by John Skinner, traveled to the mouth of the Patapsco, where they were graciously received by the fleet commander. Admiral Cochrane eventually agreed to Dr. Beanes' release. Unfortunately, due to the imminent attack on Baltimore, the party was held on board the frigate *Surprise* under the command of the Admiral's son, Sir Thomas Cochrane. On September 11, the party was transferred under guard to Key's vessel, where they were able to witness the bombardment of Fort McHenry. On the morning of the 14th, as dawn broke, the American flag still flew over the fort. Key was so surprised that he wrote "The Star Spangled Banner." Key, Beanes, and Skinner were released and the British withdrew.

That evening, in a Baltimore hotel, Key rewrote the poem, destined to become our national anthem, on the back of a letter. The next day, Key showed the letter to his brother-in-law, Joseph Nicholson, one of the defenders of Fort McHenry. Nicholson was so impressed with the poem he had it printed and distributed in handbill form. The poem first appeared in print in *The Baltimore Patriot* on September 20, 1814.

Francis Scott Key died January 11, 1843 in Baltimore and was buried in St. Paul's Church Cemetery. In 1866 his remains were moved to Mt. Olivet Cemetery and in 1898 the remains of Francis Scott Key and his wife, Mary Taylor Lloyd, were placed in the base of the Key monument, which was unveiled on August 8, 1898.

In 1916, President Woodrow Wilson made the song the official anthem of the armed forces, and on March 3, 1931, President Herbert Hoover signed the act passed by Congress making "The Star Spangled Banner" our national anthem.

*Courtesy of the Maryland Historical Society*

In early 1800, the nation was mourning the death of George Washington. Fredericktown honored him with an impressive funeral parade on February 22, 1800. Thousands were on hand to watch and pay their respects. Present in the long procession, among others, were Thomas Johnson; the governor of Maryland, Benjamin Ogle; ex-governor Thomas Sim Lee; Charles Carroll; and Lawrence Everhart, local Revolutionary War hero in Washington's army. The procession stopped at the German Presbyterian Church, where Thomas Johnson delivered a eulogy for his late friend.

By the early 1800s, Frederick was a town of about 3,000 inhabitants. Of this number, there were about 470 Negroes, 350 of whom were slaves. Frederick contained more than 400 homes, seven religious organizations, a Courthouse, and a stone jail. Frederick also contained a number of stores and was well on the way to becoming a significant manufacturing town. One of the chief industries throughout the first half of the 19th century was tanning. By 1853, there were 102,000 sides of leather being shipped from Frederick by train. In 1817, "town" was officially dropped from Frederick's name by an act of the Maryland assembly, and the city was incorporated.

Just before the War of 1812, a well-publicized trial was held in Fredericktown.

*Courtesy of Fredericktown Bank*

*Shown above is the front of the Jesuit Novitiate on East Second Street, circa 1890. The property had been sold to Father John Williams in 1765 by his friend, John Cary, for five shillings (Cary had paid more than 250 shillings for it). Father Williams built a small house on the corner of the lot in 1763, and it was used as a residence and church for nearly 40 years. Even though Catholics were able to worship publicly after the Revolution, it was 1800 before they were able to build a church in Frederick. The cornerstone, dated 15 May 1800, was unearthed in 1904 in the rubble of an alley near the site of the old novitiate and now rests in front of Saint John's Church. The church was not completed until about 1812, due to a lack of funds. In 1903 the cemetery that was established on the grounds of the novitiate was moved to Saint John's Catholic Cemetery, established in 1845 at the corner of East Third and East streets. In 1833 the novitiate buildings were considerably enlarged, due to overcrowding. At the time it was torn down in 1903, this building extended from Second to Third streets. The parish and missions were turned over to the Archdiocese of Baltimore in 1902.*

Old Stone Tavern

Courtesy of Historical Society of Frederick County, Inc.

*The Old Stone Tavern in Battletown, circa 1896, at the corner of Patrick Street and Telegraph (now Jefferson) Street, was built around 1800, prior to the opening of the National Pike. The builder and owner was a Mr. Bowers. The tavern was a haven for Henry Clay, Andrew Jackson, and Daniel Webster when they traveled on the National Pike. Folger McKinsey, the Bentztown Bard, immortalized it in his poem, "The Tavern."*

## The Tavern

*There is life in the inn, the hostlers leap
With a ruddy smile from their mountain sleep;
The Sieur de Lafayette - may be
The guest is even as great as he;
or Daniel Webster, or Jefferson,
Peers of those great days greatly won
From strife and struggle, Out gleams the light,
The Inn is revel, No sleep tonight.
Then morn, and the teamster up with the sun,
Hooked and all of his feeding done:
Ye-ho! the cumbersome wagon rolls,
Freighted with goods, and the precious souls -
Wife and babies - true pioneers,
Seeking the West of the other years,
Out of the valleys of Frederick wheat
O'er the winding way to Ohio, sweet!*

— Folger McKinsey

Brigadier General James Wilkinson, a commander in the U. S. Army, was tried by a court martial for several treasonous acts, including conspiring with Aaron Burr to take United States land west of the Allegheny Mountains and set up an empire. Defending Wilkinson were John Hanson Thomas and Roger Brooke Taney, who by this time was the best lawyer in Frederick. Both lawyers at first suspected the general's guilt and had no use for him as a person, but because

Wilkinson had taken a pauper's oath they performed their legal services free of charge. Wilkinson was acquitted after a trial that lasted three months and focused the nation's attention on the little town of Frederick.

During the War of 1812, Fredericktown was the site of much American troop movement, though it was never really in danger from the British. The town was a stopping point and staging area for troops headed to and from Washington and Balti-

more. When Washington fell in 1814, some 3,000 troops passed through Frederick on the way to both cities. Others soon followed from Frederick and Washington counties. Many men from the Frederick area were recruited for the war. During the conflict, documents and archives from Washington and money from Baltimore were deposited here for safekeeping. British prisoners from Washington were locked up in Fredericktown's jail. A British spy was

*(continued on page 38)*

*The home of Roger Brooke Taney, circa 1920, at 123 South Bentz Street, was built in 1799. Taney lived here from 1801 to 1823 with his wife, Anne. Mrs. Taney was the sister of Francis Scott Key, who visited with the Taneys often, and the home now serves as a museum for both Roger Brooke Taney and Francis Scott Key.*

Authors' Collection

*The Steiner House and doorway (above), circa 1930, located at 368 West Patrick Street, was built in 1807 by well-known architect Colonel Stephen Steiner on the brow of Bentztown Hill. It is currently the home of the Frederick Women's Civic Club and was the first home of the Historical Society of Frederick County, Inc. The seven-foot elliptical doorway has a fan glass that displays leaded tracery ornamented with flowers and tiny pineapples.*

*All Saints parish has served the Frederick community since 1742. The first church was located on All Saints Street, where Francis Scott Key attended services. The second church, shown here, circa 1890, was consecrated on November 12, 1814, on North Court Street. It was designed by local architect Henry McCleery and was built on land purchased for the parish by Phillip Thomas (son-in-law of John Hanson) and Richard Potts. The building became the parish house in 1855 upon completion of the present church on West Church Street.*

O say can you see, ~~through~~ by the dawn's early light,
What so proudly we hail'd at the twilight's last gleaming,
Whose broad stripes & bright stars through the perilous fight
O'er the ramparts we watch'd, were so gallantly streaming?
    And the rocket's red glare, the bomb bursting in air,
    Gave proof through the night that our flag was still there,
  O say does that star-spangled banner yet wave
    O'er the land of the free & the home of the brave?

On the shore dimly seen through the ~~mists~~ of the deep,
  Where the foe's haughty host in dread silence reposes,
What is that which the breeze, o'er the towering steep,
  As it fitfully blows, half conceals, half discloses?
    Now it catches the gleam of the morning's first beam,
    In full glory reflected now shines in the stream,
'Tis the star-spangled banner — O long may it wave
  O'er the land of the free & the home of the brave!

And where is that band who so vauntingly swore,
  That the havoc of war & the battle's confusion
A home & a Country should leave us no more?
  ~~Their ~~
    Their blood has wash'd out their foul footstep's pollution
  No refuge could save the hireling & slave
  From the terror of flight or the gloom of the grave,
And the star-spangled banner in triumph doth wave
  O'er the land of the free & the home of the brave.

O thus be it ever when freemen shall stand
  Between their lov'd home & the war's desolation!
Blest with vict'ry & peace may the heav'n rescued land
  Praise the power that hath made & preserv'd us a nation.
    Then conquer we must, when our cause it is just,
    And this be our motto — "In God is our trust,"
And the star-spangled banner in triumph shall wave
  O'er the land of the free & the home of the brave. —

*The original manuscript of "The Star Spangled Banner" was written on the back of a letter. The tune was taken by Key from a then-popular English drinking song, "To Anacreon in Heaven." "The Star Spangled Banner" was adopted by Congress as the national anthem in 1931, and is reproduced from the original in the possession of the Maryland Historical Society.*

*(continued from page 35)* captured in Fredericktown, probably because of the extensive military activity in the area.

When news of victory in upper Canada came in October 1814, Fredericktown celebrated. Church bells rang continuously, and the town was illuminated by a torchlight procession at night. The war officially ended in December with the signing of the Treaty of Ghent.

When word reached Frederick that the French General, Marquis de Lafayette, was planning to visit the United States in 1824, a committee of citizens invited him to come to Frederick because many local men had served under his command during the revolution. Lafayette accepted the invitation, and when he approached Frederick on December 24, 1824, he was met by Fredericktonians on the Monocacy Bridge, just outside of town. Among those present to greet him were members of the committee, Mayor Baer, several members of congress, and local Revolutionary War hero Lawrence Everhart, who had rescued the wounded Lafayette during the Battle of Brandywine. He was taken in an elaborate carriage under military escort to the hill at the head of South Market Street, where a large arch had been erected in his honor, and he was received with military honors. The procession then went on to the Courthouse, where William Ross, Esq., gave a
*(continued on page 42)*

*Dr. John Tyler built the house on West Church Street (located next to the All Saints Rectory) facing the end of Record Street in 1814, shown here as the three-story building to the right of center. He had learned that the city planned to extend Record Street, where he lived, all the way to Patrick Street, and he vehemently opposed the extension. He discovered that if a "substantial" building was placed in the path of a proposed road, the building could not be removed. Tyler built this house, and as a result, Record Street is only one block long and the house is known as the Spite House.*

*Courtesy of Fredericktown Bank & Trust*

38    CHAPTER TWO — 1800-1859

RECORD ST., FREDERICK, MD.

# RECORD STREET

Record Street is shown here, circa 1905. The house at 111 Record Street is the birthplace of William Tyler Page, author of "The American's Creed" and direct descendant of President John Tyler and Carter Braxton, a signer of the Declaration of Independence. At the time this photograph was taken, it was the home of Dr. William Crawford Johnson, who served as physician to the School for the Deaf, the Home for the Aged, and All Saints Orphanage. Dr. Johnson's wife, Ruth, was a direct descendant of President James Monroe.

The duplex located at 111 and 113 Record Street was built in 1815 by Dr. William Tyler. Both homes were severely damaged by the same fire that burned the Courthouse in 1842 and were later rebuilt. The house at 113 Record Street served as the All Saints Rectory from 1875 to 1915 and was occupied for more than 40 years by the Rev. Osborne Ingle.

At 119 Record Street is the home of Mrs. Ellen Ramsey. Here General George Hartsuff recuperated after Antietam. Abraham Lincoln called on General Hartsuff in October 1862.

William Tyler Page lived at 121 Record Street in his youth, and in 1917, he won a prize of $1,000 in an essay contest for writing the "best summary of the political faith in America."

Courtesy of Treta Mathias Michel

*Site of the the first jail in Frederick, this property, at 105 and 107 Council Street, circa 1882, was sold at auction to finance the building of a larger, more secure jail. The property was purchased in 1815 by Colonel John McPherson and his son-in-law and partner, John Brien.*

Authors' Collection

*The mirror-image homes located at 103 and 105 Council Street were designed by John and Andrew McCleery and built in 1818. The wrought iron fence was forged at Catoctin Furnace. General Robert E. Lee was quartered at 103 Council Street in September 1862, during the Confederate occupation of Frederick.*

*The fountain at the intersection of North Market and Seventh streets dates from the late 19th century. A sparsely populated East Seventh Street is in the background, circa 1880. The city Christmas tree is placed next to the fountain every year.*

*This milestone of the National Pike once indicated that there were 45 miles to Baltimore. Located on the corner of Maxwell Alley and East Patrick Street, the marker was placed there around 1820.*

*The Potts house on the corner of West Church and Court streets was built in 1818 as a two-story dwelling by Richard Potts. A third story was later added.*

(Continued from page 38)
speech and Lafayette was again honored by area military companies. After the ceremonies, the general was escorted to Colonel John McPherson's home to rest and refresh himself. An elaborate dinner at Talbott's Tavern followed.

The next morning, the general received any citizen who wished to meet and talk with him at Talbott's. That evening, a ball was held at Talbott's—probably the most famous event of its kind in Frederick. Here, the ladies finally were given an opportunity to meet Lafayette. The ball caused considerable activity among local dressmakers.

Lafayette departed for Washington on Friday morning, December 31, after a memorable visit in Frederick.

A cholera epidemic raged through the country in 1832 and hit Frederick by late August. The disease became rampant in the southern part of town, where men building the C&O Canal were closely quartered. The first death of the epidemic in Frederick was a canal laborer around the beginning of September. Before the epidemic was over, at least 100 people lay dead. Death occurred with such frequency that the undertakers were barely able to provide coffins. Deep graves were often dug and three or four caskets placed in them.

Several prominent citizens were taken by the disease, including Jacob Steiner, judge of the Orphan's Court, (Continued on page 47)

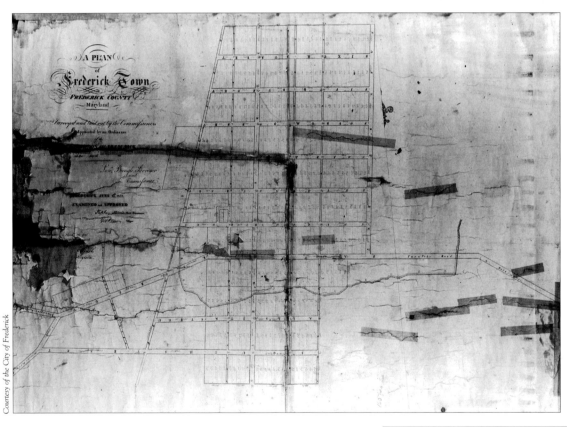

*Courtesy of the City of Frederick*

*A plan of Frederick-town, Frederick County, Maryland, prepared by Laurence Brengle, surveyor, was examined and approved by Stephen Steiner, town commissioner, and George Baer, mayor, on June 15, 1821.*

*This letter was mailed to Hagerstown, post-marked Frederick, May 5, 1826. No stamps were used.*

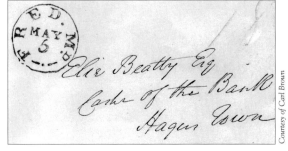

*Courtesy of Carl Brown*

PRESBYTERIAN CHURCH AND MANSE
AND HISTORIC "STONEWALL JACKSON" TREE, FREDERICK, MD.      334

*This is the United Presbyterian Church and Manse on West Second Street, circa 1890. The first church was built in 1797 on Fourth and Bentz streets. The present church was built in 1825 and dedicated in 1827, the manse about 1845. When Stonewall Jackson arrived in Frederick, he planned to attend evening church services here, conducted by his friend, J. B. Ross. Unfortunately, there were no services scheduled, so "Jackson slept" through services at the Evangelical Reformed Church. Jackson later called on the Rosses and left a note with the servants. During the Civil War, a cannonball fell through the roof and was lodged briefly in the ceiling above the pulpit.*

*General La Fayette*

# GENERAL LAFAYETTE

General Lafayette responded to the invitation of the citizens of Frederick from Baltimore. His acceptance was addressed to John McPherson, Esq., in which he acknowledged "the several testimonies of kindness, and the gratifying invitation with which I have been honored by the citizens of Frederick and County . . ."

Lafayette was concerned that he would not be able to come to Frederick and was pleased the committee was able to accommodate his schedule.

*"While I am under an obligation to stay here Tuesday night, and whats more bound to be returned to Washington City on the 31st, as the next day, January the first I must wait on the President here and have had the honor to be invited to dinner by the members of both houses of Congress. While I make ready, on Wednesday, as early as it is thought proper to depart for Frederick City, I anticipate the high satisfaction so to the citizens in which name you have done me the honor to address me and to you, Gentlemen, a tribute of my grateful and respectful thanks."*

*Lafayette*

*Quinn AME Chapel, circa 1895, founded by the Reverend William Quinn on East Third Street, was built in 1829. The African Methodist Episcopal movement was founded in Philadelphia in 1787. When Bishop Richard Allen was denied the freedom to worship in the white Methodist churches in Philadelphia, he politely left and built the first AME church on Sixth and Lombard streets in 1794. The word spread quickly and the Methodist negro members of the Frederick community worked hard to raise the money to buy the lot where their church stands and flourishes today.*

*The B&O Railroad depot was opened on December 1, 1831, at which time a ticket from Frederick to Baltimore cost $1.80. The two-story depot, located on Carroll Street, was 100 feet by 70 feet in size. In 1911, when it was torn down, it was said to be the oldest freight depot in the United States, if not the world.*

B. & O. FREIGHT DEPOT, FREDERICK, MD.
THE OLDEST RAILROAD DEPOT IN THE WORLD.

*Due to criticism of the lack of a proper ticket and passenger office in Frederick, B&O director of Frederick, T. J. Breugle, in 1854 asked the company to appropriate $5,500 for the building of a proper station. The station (left) was built on the corner of South Market Street and East All Saints Street, complete with ticket office, ladies' and gentlemen's parlors, wash rooms, and baggage rooms for the convenience of travelers. In 1948 busy rail traffic ended through the station. The building was remodeled and is now used as a community center.*

The Nallin farmhouse, now located on Fort Detrick property, was built circa 1800. This farmhouse, with its imposing double door-entrance, large door hinges and lock, front and side porches, large double-hung windows, high ceilings, and five fireplaces, captures the distinctive architecture of a pre-Civil War Maryland country home. For this reason, it was added in 1974 to the National Register of Historical Places.

Near the Nallin farmhouse is the springhouse covering the spring that is the source of a 3¹/₂-acre pond. Its stone walls are eight feet high and its dimensions are 15 feet by 16 feet. Built in 1835 of fieldstone, this springhouse served as a source of drinking water and as a cool place to store food.

The Nallin bank barn, built in 1835, is said to be designed in the style used in the late 1700s in Pennsylvania and western Maryland by Swiss and southern German settlers. Constructed of fieldstone and timber with an earth and wood floor, the barn also has a wood-framed metal and shingle roof. Legend has it that during the Civil War, both Union and Confederate troops at various times used the barn as a temporary campsite and hospital. Note that flared openings to accommodate rifle fire exist in two of the stone walls.

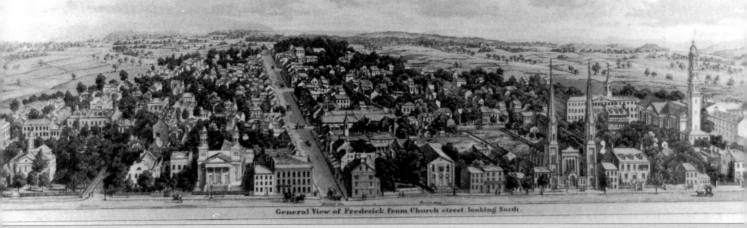

General View of Frederick from Church street, looking North.

In 1833, Charles Vaile, a civil engineer from Baltimore, wrote a book entitled
**A Complete View of Baltimore.** In this volume, he wrote:

*"Frederick City is the county town of Frederick county; it is situated on the turnpike, from Baltimore to the western county, forty-five miles from the latter city, by the turnpike road, at the end of the lateral railroad, and in the handsome valley of the Monocacy, accounted one of the most fertile in the Union. Carroll creek, a never failing stream, flows through the center of this city, and is one of indefinite service to its inhabitants for giving power to the machinery of a merchant mill, and furnishing water to several tanneries and other leather factories, all within the precincts of Frederick. It contains a handsome court-house located in a central part of the city, surrounded by both public and private stately buildings; also a jail, situated in the suburbs of the place. Here are also three banks and a savings institution; one of them is a branch of the Annapolis Bank, the other the Frederick County Bank, and the last Farmers and Mechanics Bank. Two colleges for classical education are found in this city; one called Frederick City College, located near the court-house; the professors of which are appointed by trustees, and the other is kept in a handsome building, lately erected, and under the direction of the Rev. John McElroy, a Catholic clergyman, rector of the Frederick City Catholic parish, whose usefulness has already been tested by all classes of society in that city. He receives pupils on the most accommodating terms. There is also another seminary of learning, where a complete classical education is received under the care of Mr. Woodbridge, professor of languages and mathematics. The seminary is kept in a handsome house, well situated for health, about one and one-half miles west of Frederick. Several respectable seminaries are also kept in that city for the education of young ladies, as well as a Catholic free school, where all the religious sects are admitted. It is kept by respectable ladies under the name of Sisters of Charity. Frederick is well stocked with all kinds of stores, some dry and fancy goods, and others with groceries. A large market house stands in the main street, called Market Street, and about twenty houses of public entertainment are found in this place; but the most noted, called the City Hotel, is kept by Mr. Thomas, from whence nearly all the stages depart. It is situated in this city on Patrick Street. Handsome houses of worship have been erected by several religious societies in this place; one of them by the Catholics, another by the Episcopalians, one by the German Lutherans, as well as another by the German Reformed Presbyterians, another by the Baptists, one by the Methodists, and, of late, one by the English Presbyterians.*

*The corporation has been at the expense of conveying in pipes through the city the most salubrious waters of the best springs in the mountains, one mile distant from the city, and have, last spring, placed lamps of the most approved plan in the streets, and should the improvements in private buildings keep pace with the increase of population, which is now about 5,000, this place bids fare to acquire a rank of pre-eminence among the other inland cities of the Union.*

*A line of stages start daily for Washington city, 43 miles, another for Winchester, 50 miles on the route to Staunton and hot and other springs, in Virginia; another for Wheeling, 220 miles on the road to Cincinnati, Ohio, at the reduced price of $14; another for Pittsburgh, by Hagerstown, Greencastle and Mercersburg, and another for York, on the road to Philadelphia. Several cars depart daily, at 9 a.m., for Baltimore, as well as a mail car for the same place at 8 o'clock p.m."*

(continued from page 42)

and Mr. Worley, owner of a South Market Street hotel. By late October the disease appeared to be waning. Although cholera came again the following year and in 1849 and 1854, none of these outbreaks was as serious as that of 1832.

In 1833, a financial panic spread across the nation when President Andrew Jackson ordered government funds to be withdrawn from the United States Bank. The bank was controlled by the wealthy, Jackson asserted, and he represented the people. Newly appointed Secretary of the Treasury Roger Brooke Taney carried out the president's order after the previous secretary refused. Taney also refused to re-charter the bank. As a result of the financial panic that ensued, the price of flour dropped, causing a depression in Frederick County, where growing wheat and producing flour were principal industries.

Until 1832, Frederick's streets had no lights. The only light of any kind came from taverns, shop windows, and homes, all of which were often extinguished at an early hour, "early to bed and early to rise" being the rule of the day. Nighttime travelers usually took lanterns to negotiate the still poorly paved streets. In April 1832 a town ordinance was passed, giving the town 36 street lamps. These lights, however, were dim and lit only on moonless nights. By 1850 there was a movement to light the streets (continued on page 50)

*Richfield was the home of Thomas Johnson until his wife's death in 1794 and of Admiral Winfield Scott Schley. Schley was born here in 1839 and attended the Frederick Academy and Saint John's. In 1860 he graduated from the United States Naval Academy. During the Civil War Schley served for a time under Admiral Farragut, and in 1884 he commanded the expedition to the Arctic responsible for the rescue of explorer Adolphus Greely and six members of the expedition. He was appointed rear admiral in 1898 for "conspicuous conduct in battle" during the Battle of Santiago.*

Authors' Collection

The cornerstone of the Church of Saint John the Evangelist, on the corner of Chapel Alley and East Second Street, was laid in 1833 by Father John McElroy, and the church was consecrated on April 26, 1837. Saint John's, shown here circa 1890, was the first Catholic Church in the United States to be consecrated. To the right of the church is the rectory and St. John's Literary Institute. The property across from the church was the site of the Jesuit Novitiate.

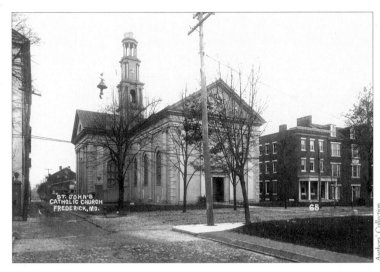

The interior of the Church of Saint John the Evangelist, circa 1895, takes the form of a Latin cross, with a 40-foot ceiling. Above the altar can be seen Galliardi's "Crucifixion," believed to be a gift to the founding Jesuits from a grateful German family.

# HARRISON

In May 1840, the Young Men's Whig Convention was held in Baltimore. One thousand young men from Frederick County marched down the turnpike from Frederick to Baltimore behind a log

cabin pulled on a wagon by six gray horses. Joining the Frederick delegation was a group from Allegany County who rolled a great ball from Cumberland. George A. Pearre was a member of this group, and he took every opportunity available to make speeches along the route.

The ball, constructed of canvas stretched over hoops and covered with rhymes, attracted a great deal of attention between Cumberland and Baltimore. At the close of the convention, it was carried to Philadelphia and rolled through the streets until it collapsed, prompting the local Democrats who witnessed it to believe it foresaw Whig candidate William Henry Harrison's defeat. However, their glee was short-lived as Harrison was elected on November 2, 1840.

On February 5, 1841, President-elect Harrison was met by a delegation of citizens headed by Col. Anthony Kimmel when he arrived by stage in Frederick. An enthusiastic crowd greeted Harrison at Dorsey's City Hotel. After dinner, the president-elect gave a brief speech to the crowd from the doorway of the hotel. He told those gathered that he was very weary and thanked the citizens of Maryland for having been among the first to nominate him. The 68-year-old walked to the train depot at 10 o'clock enroute to Baltimore. Unfortunately, the rigors of the election and his journey to Washington were more than President Harrison could endure. When he died just a few months later, many believed it was from the effects of a cold he contracted while in Frederick.

*Tyson and Son, circa 1890, fertilizer manufacturer, located on Carroll Street near the freight depot, was founded in 1842.*

*(continued from page 47)*

with gas. In spite of strong opposition to the cost, the city made a contract with the gas company for a number of lights; pipe had already been laid on the main streets of Frederick. A city ordinance was passed in January 1853 calling for 35 iron lamp posts at a cost of $19 each and requiring that the cost of gas for each post be limited to $25 per annum.

For a city of its size in the 1850s, Frederick was quite progressive in not only its street lighting improvements but also its use of water. The first waterworks dates back to 1825, when wooden pipes brought spring water 2½ miles northwest of town on Shookstown Pike to a reservoir about a mile away. This source proved inadequate, however, and in 1839, the town government looked into the matter. By late 1845 Frederick had a new water system for a cost of $90,000. ☆

*Frederick County Bank, circa 1880. The bank was founded in January 1818 with a charter granted by the General Assembly and became a national bank in 1865. Sometime during the weekend of 22-23 May 1841 the bank, located on the northwest corner of Market and Patrick streets, was robbed of $185,000. A reward of $10,000 was offered for recovery of funds and $5,000 for recovery of property.*

*In June William Wiley, a member of the New York bar and a minor court judge offered to negotiate with the robbers for a percentage of the stolen money. His offer was accepted and $164,000 worth of stolen property was returned; Wiley received a bounty of eight percent. Not long after the negotiations were completed, Wiley was involved with a similar robbery, and in December 1841 he was arrested, tried, and convicted for receiving stolen goods.*

*By J. Davis Byerly*
*Authors' Collection*

*Authors' Collection*

*Winchester Hall, shown here in the winter of 1909, was completed in 1843 on East Church Street by Hiram Winchester to house the Frederick Female Seminary. Charter and privileges were granted in 1845 and the first school catalog issued in 1846. In 1863-1864 the school was suspended, and the buildings were used as a Union hospital. In 1913, the women's college became known as Hood College when a benefactress of the school, Margaret E. Hood, died and willed $30,000 to the school. Hood College is currently located on Rosemont Avenue. Today, Winchester Hall is used by the Frederick County government.*

REFORMED CHURCH
FREDERICK, MD.

70

*Evangelical Reformed Church on West Church Street, shown here circa 1895, is the third church erected by the Evangelical Reformed congregation. The cornerstone was laid June 12, 1848, and the church was dedicated June 8, 1850. Because there were no evening services scheduled at the Presbyterian Church, General Stonewall Jackson attended evening services at the Evangelical Reformed Church on September 7, 1862. The general was accompanied by two members of his staff, Majors Douglas and Morrison. Jackson fell asleep almost immediately and did not hear the minister, Dr. Zack, offer prayers for the President of the United States.*

*Hiram Winchester planned, built, and was the first principal of the Frederick Female Seminary, erected in 1843-44. When the Frederick County government acquired the building August 1, 1931, it was renamed Winchester Hall in his honor.*

The second Court House, built in 1785, was designed by Irish immigrant Henry McCleery and was modeled after the Court of Assizes in Dublin, Ireland. As you can see from this sketch, a fire broke out in the Court House on March 31, 1842. Strong winds blew embers from the chimneys of nearby homes onto the cupola of the Court House. The fire quickly spread to many of the buildings in and around the square. The homes in the right of the picture were owned by Dr. William Tyler. They were both badly damaged by fire, but were rebuilt.

The Episcopal Orphan Home was founded in 1838 and operated for more than 100 years. The lot, purchased by Mrs. Eleanor Potts for $1,000, was located at 100 East Church Street, next to the Trail Mansion, circa 1896.

A watercolor by John Markell
shows a military encampment
held on the grounds of the
Hessian Barracks June 6-10,
1843. Companies from
Ft. McHenry, Hanover,
Hagerstown, Sharpsburg,
and Frederick participated
and were watched by large
crowds of local citizens.

Although St. John's Catholic Cemetery was not officially established until 1845, it was first used for the burial of a free black in 1832. In 1904, the graves of Roger Brooke Taney, his mother, Monica, 79 Jesuits, and others were moved from the Jesuit Graveyard to St. John's. Located at the corner of East Street and East Third Street, St. John's is the final resting place of soldiers who fought in the American Revolution, the Civil War, World Wars I and II, Korea, and Vietnam.

The third and current All Saints' Episcopal Church building
was designed by Richard Upjohn of New York, one of the
most famous architects of Gothic Revival Church architecture in America. It was completed in 1856. During the Civil
War, it was used as a hospital for the soldiers injured during
the battle of Antietam.

# VISITATION ACADEMY

Visitation Academy and Convent, located at 200 East Second Street, is shown below, circa 1890. Prior to the building of the Visitation, the grounds were used to train the militia under the direction of General "Light Horse" Harry Lee, the father of Robert E. Lee. The purpose of the militia was to train men to put down the Whiskey Rebellion in Pennsylvania in 1794. In 1823 the citizens of Frederick invited the Sisters of Charity to open an educational establishment for all denominations. When the five women arrived from Emmitsburg, they discovered they were expected to teach and live in a dilapidated log hut located on the site of the present building. The school prospered, and the log building was soon replaced by a more substantial structure of two stories. In 1845 the Sisters of Charity, who considered the care of the sick and orphans their primary duty, withdrew from the school and were replaced by the Visitation Sisters of Georgetown, who arrived on September 11, 1846. The formal enclosure was established on September 24, 1846, with Mother Mary Anastasia Combs the first Superior. The school was enlarged considerably prior to the outbreak of the Civil War. Close to 60 students were stranded at the school during the war because of the blockade, and the sisters and students were forced to reside in the convent because federal authorities commandeered the school for use as a hospital. The sisters worked tirelessly in the care of the sick and wounded. This school for girls through grade eight is primarily a boarding school, where foreign diplomats sometimes arrive to visit their children; however, a number of local young ladies attend as day students.

Authors' Collection

The altar of All Saints Episcopal Church decorated for Whitsunday, the 7th Sunday after Easter, 1882.

Courtesy of All Saints Episcopal Church

Authors' Collection

"Guess," a decorative iron dog has reclined in the doorway of All Saints' Rectory on West Church Street since the late 18th century. He has been called "Guess" since the 1840s when two sisters living there would respond with "Guess?" whenever anyone asked the dog's name. Confederate soldiers on the way to Antietam confiscated the dog to melt down for ammunition. Union soldiers found the dog abandoned in a field near Sharpsburg and returned it. Some years ago a hole was drilled in the dog's stomach to allow for the release of water, which was seriously rusting the dog.

The Rectory, built in 1790 by Dr. John Tyler, is the oldest house still standing on Court House Square. Dr. Tyler purchased the land at auction after it was confiscated from Daniel Dulany, the younger, in 1781.

# MOUNT OLIVET CEMETERY

On October 4, 1852, the Mount Olivet Cemetery Company was incorporated by the Judge of the Circuit Court for Frederick and Carroll counties. Thirty-two acres were purchased and the grounds were laid out by well-known landscape artist James Belden.

The expenses of grading, planting, general improvements, and the construction of the superintendent's lodge quickly depleted the $10,000 set aside for the cemetery. However, revenue from the sale of burial lots allowed the corporation to pay off all debts by 1862, at which time all revenue was applied to the improvement of the grounds and the acquisition of additional land.

The first president of the board was William J. Ross, Esq., who served for 25 years.

The first burial in the cemetery occurred on May 30, 1854, when Mrs. Ann Crawford was laid to rest.

*In the early 1850s, Colonel and Mrs. Charles E. Trail built this Italianate home on East Church Street. They were so strongly influenced by Italian architecture and workmanship while traveling in Italy that they commissioned Italian craftsmen to do a great deal of the work. Colonel Trail was very active in area business and government. He served as a member of Governor Bradford's staff in 1862, was a member of the House of Delegates in 1863, and was elected to the Senate in 1864. He served as president of the Women's College for 25 years and was also president of the Frederick and Pennsylvania Railway Company.*

*The first Lutherans in the area settled near the Monocacy River about ten miles north of Frederick in 1730. It is believed that by 1741 a congregation existed within Frederick, and a church was built in 1743.*

*On August 26, 1854, the cornerstone for the present Evangelical Lutheran Church on East Church Street, shown here circa 1895, was laid by the pastor, Reverend John McCron, and it was dedicated on December 8, 1855. The twin spires are 150 feet high, part of the "clustered spires" of Frederick.*

*Authors' Collection*

PICTORIAL

Roger Brooke Taney

# CHAPTER 3

# The Civil War

Chief Justice Taney Administers Oath of Office to Lincoln

Maryland Legislature Meets in Frederick to Decide on Secession

Confederate and Union Forces Move Through Frederick

Whittier Immortalizes Barbara Fritchie

Meade Succeeds Hooker as Commander of Army of Potomac

Confederate General Jubal Early Ransoms Frederick for $200,000

The Civil War came to Frederick, in a manner of speaking, in 1859. At that time, a man named Stearns canvassed the county seeking subscriptions to *Headley's Life of Washington*. Stearns was in fact John Brown's advance man, Captain Cook, who would be hung on December 16, 1859, for murder and treason after the ill-fated raid at Harpers Ferry.

News of the raid was brought to Frederick by the crew on a train that John Brown allowed to proceed, even though the crew was aware of the insurrection. Reports of the raid were misleading: The *Frederick Examiner* reported it was an insurrection by the employees at the government arsenal. The news was quickly telegraphed to Washington. Frederick's Home Brigade, composed of members of fire companies who were part of the 16th Maryland Regiment, was one of the first to volunteer its services. While the brigade was at Harpers Ferry, United Guards Captain John T. Sinn was summoned by Brown to hear his demands and accusations, and Sinn later testified at Brown's trial.

Geographically, Frederick was in the unenviable position of knowing that the city and county would become involved in the war. Basically a Southern community, Frederick was sympathetically aligned with the Southern cause, and many citizens were bitterly opposed to the abolitionists of the North. Despite *(continued on page 63)*

*"Extra" edition of the Examiner printed December 2, 1859, announcing the execution in Charlestown, Virginia, of John Brown for murder, treason, and insurrection.*

# Examiner·Extra.

## Frederick, Dec. 2d., 1859.

### Execution of JOHN BROWN, for Murder, Treason and Insurrection, at Charlestown, Va.

To gratify the public curiosity we issue, in Extra form, the following Dispatches from Charlestown, received at this office to-day.

[FIRST DISPATCH.]

CHARLESTOWN, VA., Dec'br. 2d., 1. p. m.

John Brown was hung at eleven o'clock, thirty minutes this morning. NO DISTURBANCE! He died easy; was cut down after hanging thirty-five minutes.

[SECOND DISPATCH.]

CHARLESTOWN, VA., Dec. 2d.—2 o'clock P. M.

Every thing was conducted under the strictest Military discipline, as if the town was in a state of siege. Mounted Scouts were stationed in the woods to the left of the scaffold; and Picket Guards stationed out towards the Shenandoah mountain in the rear. The Military on the field formed two hollow squares. Within the inner one was the Scaffold, and between the inner and outer lines the citizens were admitted,—none being allowed outside of the lines, except the Mounted Guards.

At Eleven o'clock, the prisoner was brought out of the Jail, accompanied by Sheriff Campbell and his assistants, and Capt. Avis, the Jailor. A wagon, containing a *white pine Coffin*, was driven up, on which the prisoner took his seat. Six companies of Infantry and Riflemen, one company of Horse, and the General and Staff, numbering 25 officers heading the procession, it moved towards the place of Execution. The prisoner was accompanied by *no ministers*, as he desired no religious ceremonies, either in Jail or on the Scaffold.

He looked calmly around on the people, perfectly self-possessed; mounted the scaffold with a firm step; his arms were pinioned by the Sheriff; bid farewell to Captain Avis and Sheriff Campbell, and at 11.30 a. m., the trap of the scaffold was pulled away, and with a few slight struggles, John Brown yielded up his spirit.

The body was placed in the coffin, and is now on its way to Harpers Ferry, to be delivered to his wife, under a strong Military escort.

*Confederate General Bradley T. Johnson's home (no longer standing), circa 1904, on the corner of West Second Street and Court Street, was purchased from Johnson by James Warfield Pearre in 1860. To the right is the home of inventor McClintock Young, Jr.*

On September 24, 1857, Thomas Holliday Hicks was one of many political candidates who spoke at an American Party rally held in Frederick. He was elected Governor of Maryland in 1857. Politically he was a conservative and was nicknamed "Old Caesar" because of his iron will. The following description of Governor Hicks appeared in the February 16, 1861 issue of Harper's Weekly: "Although now the object of severe abuse among his political opponents, on account of his conservative position, he is cordially indorsed by a large majority of the best men in Maryland; and when the smoke of the serious conflict in which we are now engaged shall roll, it will, we think, be difficult to find an unprejudiced man who will refuse to laud him for his honest efforts to avert the terrible calamities which overshadow us." In April 1861, Governor Hicks addressed the members of the Legislature in a special session held in Frederick and declared that Maryland did not have the authority to pass a resolution to secede. "We cannot but know that a large proportion of the citizens of Maryland have been induced to believe that our deliberations may result in the passage of some measure committing the State to secession. It is, therefore, our duty to declare that all such fears are without just foundation. We know that we have no constitutional authority to take such action. You need not fear that there is a possibility that we will do so. "

The property known as Kemp Hall (shown here in 1878), on the corner of Market and East Church streets, was purchased by the Reformed Church in 1762 from Christopher Lowndes. A stone parsonage was built that same year and was used until 1860, at which time the building was removed and a new parsonage with store rooms and meeting halls was erected. In 1860, when it was discovered that the old Reformed Church steeple was seriously decayed and would have to be removed, church elder Abraham Kemp strongly objected. He ordered all necessary repairs be made to save the steeple and paid $742.42 for the work. Because of this and many other generous acts, the congregation elected to name the new building Kemp Hall.

In 1861 the Maryland Legislature was about to vote on whether Maryland would or would not secede from the Union. Federal troops occupied Annapolis, and Governor Hicks, acting on President Lincoln's advice, ordered the legislature to convene in Frederick. (Lincoln feared capture of the nation's capital by Confederate forces in Virginia to the south and by Southern sympathizers in Baltimore, southern Maryland, and on the Eastern Shore.) Finding the Court House inadequate for its needs, the legislature reconvened in Kemp Hall, the Senate on the second floor and the House of Delegates on the third.

# TO THE PEOPLE OF FRED'K. COUNTY.

## FELLOW-CITIZENS,

The wide-spread prevalence of the political heresy of Secession which has resulted in the withdrawal of seven States from that Union which for nearly a century has been our pride and boast, demands our instant action, so that our silence may not be misconstrued and that our example may afford moral aid and encouragement to the loyal & patriotic men who still cling to their Country with unabated love and fidelity.

Notwithstanding the many grievances of which the South justly complains, and against which none has juster cause for remonstrance than the State of Maryland, we hold that *Secession is no remedy* for these evils, but on the contrary, is an intolerable aggravation of and an addition to them.

We hold that in a government of laws, the first duty of every citizen is obedience. That whatever injustice or wrong may be perpetrated, in a free government where the largest exercise of liberty compatible with the stability of government and the security of the people is guarantied to every individual, no such wrong or injustice can be permanent, but that a fair and candid appeal to the honesty and intelligence of the people of the whole country, will inevitably result in a full and cordial recognition of all our constitutional rights and the removal of all our existing grounds of complaint.

We hold that the temporary and accidental triumph of the Republican Party in the election of a President, while the real and substantial power of the government remained in the hands of their opponents, was no such overwhelming calamity as to compel or justify the dissolution of this Confederacy ; the total abandonment of our rights and privileges in the Union and the renunciation of the glorious heritage bequeathed to us by our Revolutionary ancestors.

We hold that the remedy for all these things is to be found, not in Secession, but at the ballot-box; and we feel justified in believing that there is already a returning sense of justice on the part of our Northern brethren.

Therefore, the undersigned earnestly invite their fellow-citizens of Frederick County, who stand by the Union of these States and oppose Secession for any past or present cause, to unite with them in

## MASS CONVENTION

### AT THE COURT HOUSE, IN THE CITY OF FREDERICK AT 10 O'CLOCK,
### ON TUESDAY, THE 26TH DAY OF MARCH, 1861

to form a Union Organization in this County and to take steps for holding a Union State Convention at an early day thereafte..

| | | | | | |
|---|---|---|---|---|---|
| Jacob Bear | Otho Norris | Jacob Sahm | Ephraim Creager | Lewis H. Bennett, | Daniel S. Loy, |
| R. Potts | J D Getzendanner | Jacob Reifsnider | Spencer C Jones | P. Jefferson Hawman, | William Dean, |
| L. J. Brengle | Ulysses Hobbs | Charles E Mealey | Grafton W Elliott | Lloyd Dorsey, | W. H. C. Dean, |
| John Loats | Charles Cole | Charles W Haller | John Poole | Robert Shafer, | Josiah Harrison, |
| Chas E Trail | J A Simmons | Frederick Main | Frederick Kehler | George W. Summers, | Harrison Conley, |
| Wm P Maulsby | Frederick Keefer | Geo C Johnson | Jacob Detre | Henry C. Steiner, | Nicholas T. Haller, |
| James Cooper | Christian Steiner | Charles Mantz | Wilson R Boyd | John J. Kantner, | L. M. Englebrecht, |
| Frederick Schley | Charles Lease | E Y Goldsborough | Erasmus West | Lawrence Bentz, | James W. Phebus, |
| Grayson Eichelberger | James T Smith | Samuel R Hogg | L V Scholl | Daniel A. Staley, | C Getzendanner, |
| James Whitehill | D C Winebrenner | Jacob Fox | G R Kephart | Anthony Kimmel, | John T. Martin, |
| Edward Shriver | James Hopwood | David Weaver | Daniel H Rohr | Francis T. Rhodes, | Henry Lorentz, |
| Adam Wolfe | Barney Fisher | Wm Johnston | George K Birely | George W. Derr, | William Lorentz, |
| Nicholas Whitmore | James Hergesheimer | Edward Trail | D W Brooks | Isaac P. Suman, | John Routzahn, |
| Wm D Reese | Zephaniah Harrison | W G Moran | John Lyeth | George W. L. Bartgis | Mathias Ahalt, |
| J W L Carty | A Gault | Daniel Haller | I W Suman | John Wilson | John Sifford, |
| Basil Norris | Edward Buckey | George Engelbrecht | C T Albaugh | George Gittinger | Geo T. Williard, |
| W Tyler, Sr | Thos M Holbrunner | Thomas M Markell | John T Schley | James Bruner | Thomas Hooper, |
| Jacob Markell | John Mackechney | William T Haller | Isaiah Mealey | H. K. Hilton | John Cramer, |
| R Y Stokes | Edward Sinn | John E Sifford | John Sanner | Michael Englebrecht | James W. Hood, |
| John Schreiner | Val S Brunner | John Goldsborough | George S Groshon | William Glessner, | J George Sinn, |
| R H Macgill | Wm G Cole | George F Webster | John H Mumford | George Kantner, | J. R. Marken, |
| P L Storm | Tobias Haller | G W Delaplane | Robert Boone, | A. H. Hunt, | John Hooper, |
| W B Tyler | Jacob Himmell | Daniel Sweadner | David Boyd, Sr., | Thos. T. Cromwell, | William Hooper, |
| Francis Markell | John J Woodward | E Albaugh | Levi Vanfossen, | W. R. Sanderson, | James Hooper, |
| P M Englebrecht | L M Schaeffer | George W. Ulrich | Dennis Scholl, | W. J. Lynn Smith, | W. H. R. Kelty, |
| George Markell | Wm G Schaeffer | Abraham Haff | William H. Brish, | Simon Parsons, | O. F. Butler, |
| Lewis Markell | M Keefer | Charles E Albaugh | Isacher Himbury, | Frederick Shipley, | Gideon Bantz, |
| Emanuel Mantz | T J McGill | D T Runner | William Higgins, | Abraham Kemp, | David Kenega, |
| John Ramsburgh, | George Salmon, | Andrew Boyd, | Richard T. Dixon | George M. Tyler, | Upton Buhrman, |
| Jacob Knauff, | Jonathan T. Wilson, | Hiram H. Mullen | Lewis H. Dill, | Maurice Albaugh, | W. L. Hays, |
| George A. Abbott, | William H. James, | John H. Abbott, | John J. Suman, | William T. Duvall, | A. E. Smith, |

| | | | | | | | |
|---|---|---|---|---|---|---|---|
| John McPherson, | Wm. B. Tabler, | W. Lochner, | Fairfax Schley, | Grafton Fout, | Charles W. Eader, | Jacob Ramsburg, | Clark Eldridge, |
| Saml. B. Preston, | Wm. T. Gittings, | R. G. McPherson, | Hiram M. Nusz, | George Metzger, | Jacob Leilich, | George Buhrman, | M. G. Arnold, |
| Dewalt Williard, | Isaac Keller, | William Stokes, | John T. Martin, | Adam Custard, | Michael H. Haller, | Henry C. Frazier, | Hanson T. C. Green |
| Samuel Carmack, | Wm. T. Preston, | B. A Cunningham, | N. D. Hauer, | G. W. Dertzbaugh, | John Stimmel, | William Mahony, | J. J. Moran, |
| J. McPherson, of W | James Williamson, | John H. Keller, | John S. Burucker, | T. E. Getzendanner | Charles W. Miller, | John H. Young, | George R. Dennis, |
| Sebast'n Ramsburg, | Wm. H. Derr, | James M. Harding, | John Fauble, | Benjamin Ebert, | Benjamin Routzahn | B. G. Fitzhugh, | Dr; J. Bonne, |
| Jacob Grove, | John M. Ebert, | Henry M. Nixdorf, | G. P. Ramsburg, of J | H. F. Schindler, | George D. Miller, | Henry Schley, | L. A. Brengle, Jr. |
| Jacob Riehl, | William H. Grove, | Henry B. Fessler, | John T. Moore, | Samuel Haller, | A. P. Kessler, | A. H. Reinhart, | G. J. Doll, |
| John T. Green, | David K. Schaeffer, | Samuel B. Ebert, | Mason R. Marsh, | George W. Custard, | William H. Rice, | Christian Woerner, | Isaac Wisong, |
| Hiram Schissler, | Charles H Keefer, | Chas. E. Campbell, | Lewis Medtart, | N. H. Pitts, | Henry A. Cole, | George Hoskins, | T. M. Morgan, jr. |
| Philip Cramer, | George W Cramer, | Philip H Sinn; | Edward Young. | | | | |

*Printed at the Office of "The Maryland Union" Frederick, Md.* [March 19, 1861.]

*Original Owned By*
BERGER'S BOOK MART
*Frederick, Maryland*

*A circular printed by The Maryland Union in Frederick announced a mass convention to be held at the Court House on March 26, 1861. The purpose of the convention was to show opposition to secession and support of the Union.*

*Courtesy of Fredericktown Bank & Trust*

(continued from page 60)

these sentiments, the citizens were, for the most part, staunchly opposed to secession as a means of solving the problems and remained fiercely loyal to the Union.

During the November 1860 presidential election, 3,617 citizens sympathetic to slavery voted for the Democratic candidate John Bell; 3,609 supported the Whig platform in favor of maintaining the Union, by voting for Stephen Douglas. Only 103 citizens of the county voted for Abraham Lincoln. Voters were so closely divided that a county convention was called on December 17, 1860, to decide the issues. A voice vote was impossible; therefore, it was decided that those in favor of the Union would pass through the east gate of the Court House; those in favor of secession, the south gate. When all had made their choice, 341 passed through the east gate; 117, the south gate.

Shortly before the governor convened the legislature in Frederick, the Maryland General Assembly instructed Governor Thomas Holliday Hicks to order the militias throughout the state to return all arms issued by the state. The Frederick Home Guard refused, as did most others in the state, and fearing violence, the governor rescinded the order.

Many members of the legislature hoped to force the passage of a bill of secession. However, letters were intercepted by federal authorities, and the secretary of war

Chief Justice Roger Brooke Taney administered the oath of office to Abraham Lincoln in 1861. Taney also administered the oath to Presidents Van Buren, Harrison, Polk, Taylor, Pierce, and Buchanan.

ordered Maryland to remain in the Union at all cost. As a result, when the legislature reconvened here in September, military authorities and police from Baltimore surrounded the city and searched it, arresting a total of 22 people—14 legislators and 8 citizens. Those arrested were taken to Baltimore by train and held for a time at Fort McHenry, then later transferred to Fort Lafayette in Boston Harbor.

In May 1861, one of the many companies containing Frederick citizens, the First Regiment of Infantry, was organized in Baltimore, consisting of men from Baltimore, Howard, and Frederick counties. It was involved in the bloody battle at Front Royal, Virginia, on May 23, 1862, where a great many of the men fell. The First Regiment fought bravely throughout the war and was present on September 9, 1865, when General Robert E. Lee surrendered at Appomattox.

By the end of 1861, 15,000 Union troops were quartered in Frederick. The provost marshal was quartered in Kemp Hall, and the federal government paid rent to the Reformed Church for use of the building until 1866. Kemp Hall was also used as a military supply depot; it took 500 wagon loads of supplies to stock it initially.

In 1862 the federal government chose the Hessian Barracks as the site of the Union Military Hospital, one of the largest hospital centers in the Union. Dr. R.F. Weir (continued on page 67)

*Authors' Collection*

*The United States Hospital was established on the grounds surrounding the old barracks at the top of South Market Street in August 1861 by Brigadier General Nathaniel Banks.*

*When Stonewall Jackson entered the city on September 10, 1862, his troops passed down Mill Alley (now Bentz Street) and crossed over the swinging bridge to Patrick Street. The stone mill to the left is the old Zentz Mill, c. 1790. The bridge, still in use today, has been moved twice. It was first relocated to a point near the Baker Park Carillon. It was moved again in 1930 to its present location (between the end of Jefferson Street and the municipal swimming pool, for the opening of Parkway School.*

*Courtesy of the Historical Society of Frederick County,*

## Head-Quarters, City Guard,
### OFFICE of the PROVOST MARSHAL,
#### Frederick City, December 16th, 1861.

THE following Orders are published for the information of all Concerned:

**1st.** Soldiers found in the City of Frederick without proper passes will be immediately arrested and confined in the Guard House.

**2d.** All passes granted by commanding officers for a longer time than one day, or after sundown of that day, are void and will be taken from the persons having them.

**3d.** All soldiers found in the City of Frederick after sundown will be placed in confinement under charge of the guard unless on pass countersigned by the Assistant Adjutant-General at Division Head-Quarters.

**4th.** All soldiers are forbidden to congregate in Hotels, Drinking Saloons or other public places, or to collect on the street corners, or in any way to obstruct the sidewalks.

**5th.** All persons connected with the army who are guilty of disorderly or improper conduct will be arrested and punished according to the nature of their offence, by Court Martial or otherwise.

**6th.** The pickets upon the roads leading into the city, will stop all soldiers without passes, and destroy liquor found in the possession of soldiers.

**7th.** The rules and orders in relation to the use of ambulances will be strictly enforced.

**8th.** All teamsters of Government wagons will drive their teams no faster than a walk; will take the right hand side of the street; will not stop on crosswalks or elsewhere on the street, and will be careful in the driving of their teams, and in no case will one team be driven side by side with another. All teamsters offending against any of the above rules will be suitably punished.

**9th.** All persons are forbidden to drive or ride in the streets in a fast or reckless manner.

**10th.** All persons, and especially keepers of Hotels and Saloons, are forbidden to sell or give liquor to soldiers. If soldiers are found intoxicated in such public places, the keepers thereof will be considered as keepers of disorderly houses and treated accordingly.

**11th.** All ordinances of the City of Frederick having in view the maintenance of peace and good order, will be rigidly enforced.

### THOS. H. RUGER,
Dec. 16th., 1861.           Col. 3d. Wis. Vols., Provost Marshal.

*Printed by Schley, Heller & Co., The Examiner Power Presses, Frederick Town, Md.*

*Rules and orders governing Union soldiers when in Frederick city were issued by Colonel Thomas H. Ruger, provost marshal, December 16, 1861.*

The Evangelical Lutheran Church was one of many Frederick buildings used as a hospital during the Civil War. Pictured here are soldiers wounded during the Battle of Antietam, September 1862. Wooden planks were placed over the pews to protect them and cots were placed on the planks.

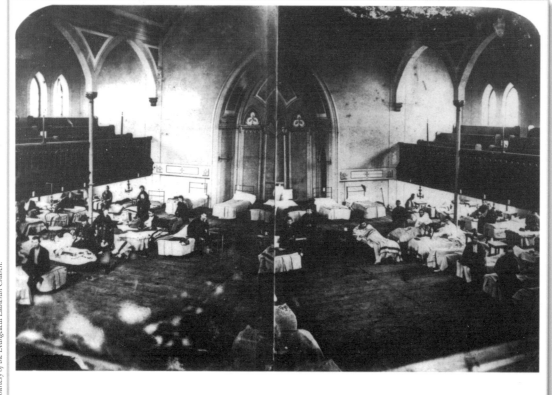

(continued from page 64)
was the administrator of this hospital, which was eventually capable of caring for as many as 900 wounded at a time.

Lee camped outside Frederick on September 6, 1862. With him were many Maryland natives who had been away from home for a long time and were ecstatic to be on Maryland soil again. Prior to the arrival of the Confederates, many area residents fled, and the supply depot was emptied. Lee's men were poorly clothed and in need of food. For the most part, they were able to obtain what they needed, paying for their supplies with Confederate money, as they were under orders to do. Stonewall Jackson also camped on the outskirts of Frederick at this time and was soon to be involved in an incident that would bring fame to Barbara Fritchie.

While the 80,000 Confederates were here, martial law was declared and Colonel Bradley T. Johnson of Frederick was appointed provost marshal. The Confederates had hoped many area citizens would volunteer to join them, but few did. They left as quickly as they came, with Union General George B. McClellan hot on their heels.

On September 14, 1862, the Battle of South Mountain occurred—a battle so fierce it could be heard in Frederick. Two days later, the forces of Lee and McClellan met again, in the bloody two-day Battle of Antietam. Casualties numbered 23,000 on both sides (more than one-fifth of the (continued on page 70)

*Confederate soldiers passed Joseph Rosenstock's Dry Good and Clothing Store at the corner of Patrick and Market streets in September 1862.*

Courtesy of the Historical Society of Frederick County, Inc.

*Courtesy of Paul and Rita Gordon*

*Union troops in front of City Hall prepared to march in a parade on North Market Street.*

*Union troops marched in a parade up Market Street in honor of President Washington's birthday in 1862.*

# ABRAHAM LINCOLN

A large crowd gathered at the B&O station to see President Abraham Lincoln depart for Washington on October 4, 1862. The president had conferred with General George B. McClellan after the Battle of Antietam. His party traveled across South Mountain by Army ambulance, and upon reaching Frederick, the president stopped at the Record Street home of Mrs. Ramsey to visit with General George L. Hartsuff, who was recuperating there from his wounds.

Before departing, President Lincoln responded to the warm reception he had received by addressing the citizens of Frederick:

"Fellow Citizens: I see myself surrounded by soldiers and by the citizens of this good city of Frederick, all anxious to hear something from me. Nevertheless, I can only say — as I did elsewhere five minutes ago — that it is not proper for me to make speeches in my present position. I return thanks to our gallant soldiers for the good service they have rendered, the energies they have shown, the hardships they have endured, and the blood they have so nobly shed for this dear Union of ours. And I also return thanks, not only to the soldiers, but to the good citizens of Frederick, and to all the good men, women, and children throughout this land for their devotion to our glorious cause. And I say this without any malice in my heart towards those who have done otherwise. May our children, and our children's children, for a thousand generations, continue to enjoy the benefits conferred upon us by a united country, and have cause yet to rejoice under those glorious institutions bequeathed us by Washington and his compeers! Now, my friends — soldiers and citizens — I can only say once more — farewell!"

*Authors' Collection*

*Authors' Collection*

(continued from page 67)

total forces), and most were cared for in the hospitals in Frederick city and county until they were well enough to be moved to Baltimore or Washington by train. At this time there were 20 hospitals in the city, serving more than 4,000 meals and moving 700 wounded north each day.

On October 1, 1862, President Lincoln arrived in Frederick after conferring with General McClellan and touring the battlefields at South Mountain and Antietam. In Frederick he visited the wounded General Hartsuff and before leaving spoke to a large crowd gathered in the rain at the train station. Lincoln thanked his soldiers for their sacrifices and the citizens of Frederick and the nation for their "devotion in the glorious cause."

In September 1863, after the Battle of Gettysburg, the Frederick hospitals were again filled to capacity.

On the morning of July 7, 1864, rumors began circulating among the citizens of Frederick that the Confederates, under the command of General Jubal Early, were in the vicinity of Middletown and would soon reach Frederick and attempt to occupy the city. Before long, couriers as well as wounded began arriving. By noon that day, businesses had closed and many people had fled the city. Citizens were concerned about their safety because only Colonel Clendenin's troops were present in the city. By four o'clock the Confederate troops could be seen

from many rooftops. Several skirmishes occurred over the next two days, and the Union troops finally withdrew. By the time the Confederate troops entered the city, much of the stores and supplies were gone, having been removed by the Union troops. After the Confederates' arrival, a letter was delivered to Mayor Cole demanding the payment of $200,000 for the use of the army of General Early. Through the endeavors of the mayor and the cooperation of the banks in the city, the money was raised and delivered to General Early. While Early was waiting for the payment of the ransom, some of his soldiers obtained food and other supplies locally. But unlike Lee's troops, they refused to pay.

After General Early received the ransom money, he left Frederick heading south, with his main objective to surprise and seize Washington, D.C. In the meantime, Union troops were massing on a six-mile line along the Monocacy River. General Lew Wallace and 5,000 Union soldiers, more than half untried in battle, were waiting at the Monocacy Bridge, three miles south of the city. A short vicious battle lasting from 11 a.m. until 5 p.m. took the lives of 398 men and wounded 1,038. General Early then proceeded toward Washington, but he was too late. General Ulysses S. Grant had fortified the city, and Early hastily headed to Virginia by way of Poolesville, then across the Potomac.

*(continued on page 75)*

*This depiction of Frederick from atop South Market Street was printed in Harper's Weekly at the time of the first Confederate invasion of the city in 1862.*

*Courtesy of Richard Lebherz*

*Thomas Jonathan "Stonewall" Jackson was the "nemesis" of Barbara Fritchie. Although it is doubtful that the events described in Whittier's poem actually occurred, it is known that Jackson attended evening services at the Evangelical Reformed Church on Sunday, September 7, 1862. After leaving Frederick, Jackson and his men went on to capture the fortress at Harpers Ferry, and fight at Antietam and Fredericksburg. On May 2, 1863, his march through the Wilderness helped make Lee's victory at Chancellorsville possible. That evening, Jackson was wounded by "friendly fire" when his party was mistaken for Yankees and he suffered the loss of an arm. Jackson should have recovered from his wounds, but he contracted pneumonia and died. Robert E. Lee paid tribute to Jackson when he said "I know not how to replace him."*

*Authors' Collection*

# BARBARA FRITCHIE

Barbara Hauer Fritchie, immortalized as the heroine of John Greenleaf Whittier's poem, was born on December 3, 1766, in Lancaster, Pennsylvania. She moved to Frederick as a young girl and spent the rest of her life here. In 1791, when George Washington spent the night at Mrs. Kimbal's Hotel, her Liverpool china was used to serve his dinner. At the "Memorial" funeral procession for Washington held in Frederick, she was one of the pallbearers.

She married John Casper Fritchie, fourteen years her junior, on May 6, 1806. Although her husband's father was Casper Fritchie, a convicted Tory who was executed on August 17, 1781, John was a respected member of the community and a successful glove maker.

Barbara Fritchie died at the age of 96, on December 18, 1862, and was buried next to her husband in the Reformed Graveyard on Bentz Street. Because so many visitors came to see the relics of John Greenleaf Whittier's heroine, her niece, Mrs. John Abbott, placed a book in her parlor for the visitors to sign. The first person to sign the register was 80-year-old Henry Beaver of Conshohocken, Pennsylvania, who had marched past the house with General Reno on September 12, 1862, and had seen Barbara proudly waving her flag.

Two days after the "incident" with Stonewall Jackson, General Reno passed with his troops on the way to the Battle of South Mountain, a battle from which the general would not return. When Reno saw her, he rode up and spoke to her and asked for her flag, but she said she could not bear to part with it. However, she did present him with a larger one. When Reno died, the flag was found on his body and was sent to his family in Massachusetts. While he visited with her, Barbara gave the general a glass of her homemade wine, and the wine set is now on display, minus one glass. Mrs. Abbott sent that glass to Whittier on his last birthday, along with a photograph of the famous flag.

TOMB OF BARBARA FRITCHIE, OLD REFORMED GRAVE YARD, FREDERICK, MD.

331

Sketch of John Greenleaf Whittier. Inspired by a third hand account
of the incident involving Barbara Fritchie, Whittier wrote a poem
which was first published in The Atlantic Monthly in October 1863.
When Whittier died in 1892 at the age of 84, he was one of
America's most beloved poets.

*Authors' Collection*

*Authors' Collection*

# BARBARA FRITCHIE*

*A Poem By John Greenleaf Whittier*

Up from the meadows rich with corn,
Clear in the cool September morn,

The clustered spires of Frederick stand,
Green-walled by the hills of Maryland

Round about them orchards sweep
Apple and peach tree fruited deep.

Fair as a garden of the Lord
To the eyes of the famished rebel horde.

On that pleasant morn of the early fall
When Lee marched over the mountain-wall,

Over the mountains winding down
Horse and foot into Fredericktown.

Forty flags with their silver stars,
Forty flags with their crimson bars.

Flapped in the morning wind; the sun
Of noon looked down, and saw not one.

Up rose Barbara Fritchie then,
Bowed with fourscore years and ten;

Bravest of all in Frederick-town,
She took up the flag the men hauled down:

In her attic window the staff she set,
To show that one heart was loyal yet.

Up the street came the rebel tread,
Stonewall Jackson riding ahead.

Under his slouched hat left and right
He glanced, the old flag met his sight.

"Halt!" — the dust-brown ranks stood fast.
"Fire!" — out blazed the rifle-blast;

It shivered the window, pane and sash;
It rent the banner with seam and gash.

Quick as it fell, from the broken staff
Dame Barbara snatched the silken scarf,

She leaned far out on the window sill,
And she shook it forth with a royal will.

"Shoot if you must, this old gray head,
But spare your country's flag," she said.

A shade of sadness, a blush of shame,
Over the face of the leader came,

The nobler nature within him stirred
To life at that woman's deed and word,

"Who touches a hair of your gray head,
Dies like a dog! March on!" he said.

All day long through Frederick street
sounded the tread of the marching feet.

All day long that free flag tost
Over the heads of the rebel host.

Ever its torn folds rose and fell
On the loyal winds that loved it well;

And through the hill gaps sunset light
Shone over it with a warm good night.

Barbara Fritchie's work is o'er
And the rebel rides on his raids no more.

Honor to her! and let a tear
Fall, for her sake, on Stonewall's bier.

Over Barbara Fritchie's grave
Flag of freedom and Union, wave!

Peace and order and beauty draw
Round the symbol of light and law.

And ever the stars above looked down
On thy stars below in Frederick-town..

***\* Whittier actually spelled his heroines name "Frietchie."***

# ROBERT E. LEE

While camped near Frederick, Robert E. Lee, commanding general of the Confederate Army of Northern Virginia, wrote the following on 8th September 1862:

"To the People of Maryland: It is right that you should know the purpose that has brought the Army under my command within the limits of your State, so far as that purpose concerns yourselves.

The people of the Confederate States have long watched with the deepest sympathy the wrongs and outrages that have been inflicted upon the citizens of a Commonwealth, allied to the States of the South by the strongest social, political and commercial ties.

They have seen with profound indignation their sister state deprived of every right, and reduced to the condition of a conquered Province.

Under the pretense of supporting the Constitution, but in violation of its most valuable provisions, your citizens have been arrested and imprisoned upon no charge, and contrary to all forms of law; the faithful and manly protest against this outrage made by the venerable and illustrious Marylander to whom in better days, no citizen appealed for right in vain, was treated with scorn and contempt; the government of your chief City has been usurped by armed strangers; your Legislature has been dissolved by the unlawful offences (sic) by an arbitrary decree of the Federal Executive, and citizens ordered to be tried by a military commission for what they may dare to speak.

Believing that the People of Maryland possessed a spirit too lofty to submit to such a government, the people of the South have long wished to aid you in throwing off this foreign yoke, to enable you again to enjoy the inalienable rights of freemen, and restore independence and sovereignty to your State.

In obedience to this wish, our Army has come among you, and is prepared to assist you with the power of its arms in regaining the rights of which you have been despoiled.

This, Citizens of Maryland, is our mission, so far as you are concerned.

No constraints upon your free will is intended; no intimidation will be allowed.

Within the limits of this Army at least, Marylanders shall once more enjoy their ancient freedom of thought and speech.

We know no enemies among you, and will protect all of every opinion.

It is for you to decide your destiny, freely and without constraint.

This army will respect your choice whatever it may be, and while the Southern people will rejoice to welcome you to your natural position among them, they will only welcome you when you come of your own free will."

*Authors' Collection*

On September 13, 1862, Private B.W. Mitchell and Sergeant J. M. Bloss, members of Company E of the 27th Indiana, were given orders to stack arms and take a break in a field outside Frederick that had recently been held by the Army of Northern Virginia, commanded by Robert E. Lee. Sergeant Bloss found a large envelope in the grass that contained three cigars wrapped in an official looking document. While Bloss tried to locate a match, Private Mitchell glanced at the document and discovered that it was from the Headquarters, Army of Northern Virginia, Special Order 191, by the Command of General R. E. Lee: R. H. Clinton, Assistant Adjutant-General. The men immediately turned the envelope over to their commanding officer, and the envelope and its contents were taken to division headquarters and Bloss and Mitchell returned to the empty field, without the cigars. Initially it was believed that the document was a hoax, but one of the staff officers recognized Chilton's handwriting. Unfortunately, a Confederate sympathizer was present when the order was being discussed, and he quickly rode west to inform General Stuart, who passed the information on to Lee. (Photo of Lee seated with unidentified members of his staff)

*Authors' Collection*

(continued from page 71)

The Battle of the Monocacy, ignored by many historians and given mere footnotes by others, was crucial. If it had not occurred and if Early had been able to move on Washington unmolested, the Union forces protecting Washington might not have had time to prepare an adequate defense of the city. Or, if they had been able to defend the city, they might have captured General Early. Either way, without the Battle of the Monocacy, the course of the war, not to mention the history of our nation, might have been altered.

After the Battle of the Monocacy, when union troops learned that Southern sympathizers had furnished the Confederates with information about troop size, movement, and location, the troops quartered in Frederick began a campaign to punish local sympathizers. All male citizens were required to sign an oath of allegiance to the Union, and those who refused were imprisoned and had their property seized.

When the war finally ended in April 1865, the citizens of Frederick went wild with joy. Stores closed, church bells rang continuously, homes were decorated with flowers and illuminated late into the night, and the city was decorated with flags. The joy was short-lived, however, for on April 14 President Lincoln was assassinated, and the nation mourned. ☆

A call for volunteers was issued by the Confederate Army on September 8, 1862. In the circular, Colonel Bradley T. Johnson stated: "After sixteen months of oppression more galling than the Austrian tyranny, the Victorious Army of the South brings freedom to your doors."

*A military tribunal was conducted in Frederick, in December 1862.*

*The participants were:*
1) *Capt. Lyeth, 1st Maryland;*
2) *Major Dallam, 7th Maryland;*
3) *Lt. Damuth, 6th Maryland;*
4) *Capt. Prentiss, 6th Maryland;*
5) *Lt. Vasseum, 12th Illinois Cavalry;*
6) *Lt. Haws, 7th Maryland;*
7) *Capt. Larrabee, 8th Maryland;*
8) *Lt. Edward Y. Goldsborough, Judge Advocate, 8th Maryland.*

*General George McClellan arrived in Frederick in September 1862, in pursuit of General Robert E. Lee. The campaign would lead to battles at South Mountain and Antietam, in which Lee would be forced to abandon his northern invasion.*

*Prior to Gettysburg, the Army of the Potomac, led by General Joseph Hooker (far left), camped in the area of Prospect Hall (shown above). General Hooker felt that his ability to command his troops was being hampered by Washington. When his request to withdraw the garrison at Harpers Ferry was denied, he resigned his command. The War Department wasted no time in accepting the resignation. Early in the morning of June 28, 1863, General George Meade (immediate left) was awakened by an official of the War Department and informed that he had been chosen to replace Hooker as the Commander of the Army of the Potomac.*

# JUBAL A. EARLY

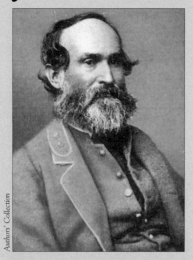

General Jubal A. Early, received $200,000 in ransom money from Frederick during a campaign in which his army threatened and almost captured Washington, DC, in July 1864.

Because of his skills as an aggressive and bold fighter, Early was placed in charge of all Confederate forces in the Shenandoah Valley, protecting Richmond, in the summer of 1864 by General Robert E. Lee. Lee had mapped out a northern invasion strategy for Early that he hoped would relieve the great Union pressure on his forces at Richmond and also, perhaps, gain a political victory that would end the war in a negotiated peace.

The political stakes were very high in that summer of 1864, and the war hung in the balance. Union forces were still fighting to capture Richmond and Atlanta. A Northern peace movement that grew stronger with each day's casualty lists threatened Lincoln's reelection in November 1864. European recognition and intervention on the side of the Confederacy was still a possibility.

This was the context in which Lee sent Early north. He was to remove Union forces from the Shenandoah Valley, cross the Potomac River into western Maryland, and finally head toward Washington to wreak havoc and capture the city. Early accomplished many of his objectives, but arrived at the Union capital too late, after a delaying and costly battle just south of Frederick along the Monocacy River allowed Union relief forces from Virginia to arrive in time to defend the city.

After Early withdrew to Virginia, he was involved in a series of defeats in the Shenandoah Valley campaigns of late 1864 and early 1865 at the hands of General Philip Sheridan, who was sent by General Ulysses S. Grant to neutralize the valley once and for all. These defeats led to the fall of Richmond and Lee's eventual surrender at Appomattox Courthouse in April 1865.

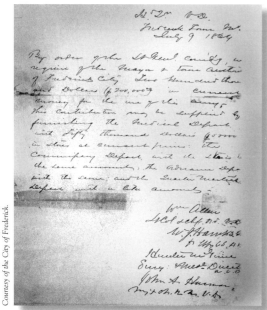

The following is the famous order of General Jubal A. Early, issued July 9th, 1864, demanding $200,000 from the citizens of Frederick to save the town from destruction:

"We require of the Mayor and town authorities two hundred thousand dollars ($200,000) in current money for the use of this army. This contribution may be supplied by furnishing the medical department with fifty thousand dollars ($50,000) in stores at current prices, the commissary department with stores to the same amount, the ordnance department with the same and the quartermaster department with a like amount.

Signed:

Wm. Allen, Lieut.-Col. and Chief Ord. V.D.
W.D. Hawks, Chief Com., C. S. A., O.D.
Hunter McGuire, Surg. and Med. Director
John A. Horman, Maj. and Chief Q.M., V.D.

A list of the stores originally requested from Frederick by General Early for the use of his troops.

A letter dated July 9, 1864 to General Early from Mayor Cole requested that the general reconsider the assessment imposed upon the citizens of Frederick, arguing that it was much higher than other communities were required to pay and that it would "take from the citizens of this place nearly one tenth of the taxable property of the city."

The following is a transcription of the resolution (above) passed by the city government.

Whereas, the Lieut. General Commanding the Confederate Army now occupying this Town has made a demand on the Corporate authorities for the sum of Two hundred thousand dollars ($200,000).

And whereas, at a meeting of the Corporate authorities of said Town held this day, the following proceedings were had, with the concurrence and approval of the Citizens present,

Resolved by the Mayor, Aldermen & Common Council of Frederick, That the several Banking and Savings Institutions of the Town be requested to furnish so much of said sum of Two hundred thousand dollars pro rata according to their several & respective abilities and that the Corporate authorities will proceed at the earliest possible moment to reimburse said Banks and Savings Institutions, by levying upon the Citizens of said Corporation in proportion to their ability a sufficient tax to cover the same.

Resolved by the authority aforesaid, That the Mayor, Messrs. Sifford, Brunner, of the Board of Aldermen, Jno. A. Simmons & T. M. Holbruner of the Board of Com. Council & Joseph Baugher, R. H. Marshall, Lewis M. Nixdorf, Calvin Page and E. Albaugh, Esq. be authorized to demand said funds & pay over the same to the proper officer of said Army.

Based upon their assets, the local banks contributed money toward the ransom: Farmers and Mechanics, $28,000; Franklin Savings Bank, $31,000; Frederick County Bank, $33,000; Central Bank, $44,000; and Fredericktown Savings Institution, $64,000. The $200,000 in greenbacks was collected by city officials, loaded into baskets, and transported by wagon to the Confederate officials.

The circular image with text:

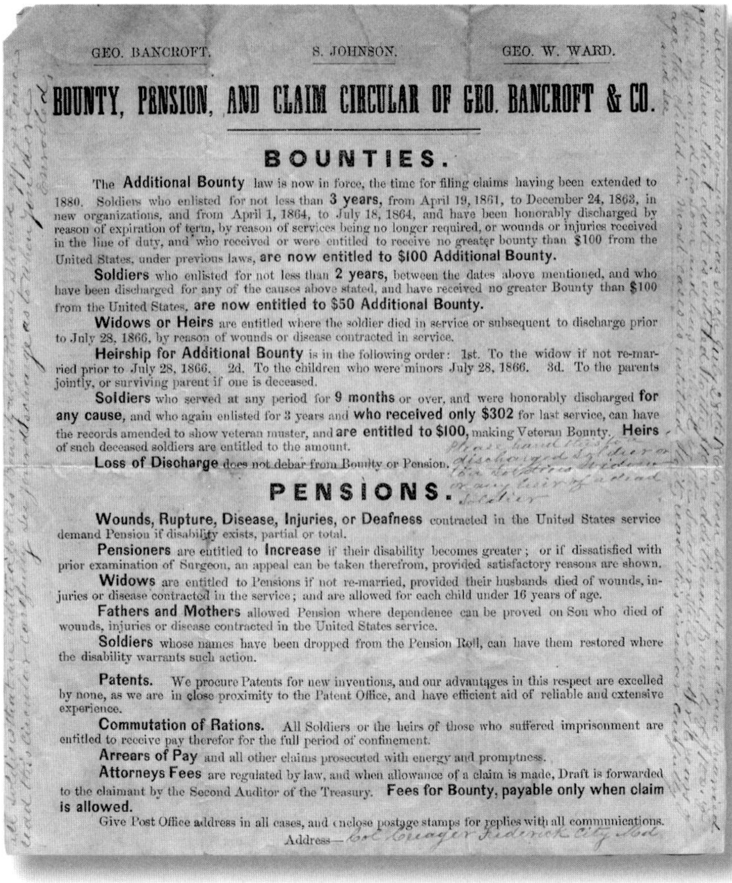

GEO. BANCROFT.   S. JOHNSON.   GEO. W. WARD.

# BOUNTY, PENSION, AND CLAIM CIRCULAR OF GEO. BANCROFT & CO.

## BOUNTIES.

The **Additional Bounty** law is now in force, the time for filing claims having been extended to 1880. Soldiers who enlisted for not less than **3 years**, from April 19, 1861, to December 24, 1863, in new organizations, and from April 1, 1864, to July 18, 1864, and have been honorably discharged by reason of expiration of term, by reason of services being no longer required, or wounds or injuries received in the line of duty, and who received or were entitled to receive no greater bounty than $100 from the United States, under previous laws, **are now entitled to $100 Additional Bounty.**

**Soldiers** who enlisted for not less than **2 years**, between the dates above mentioned, and who have been discharged for any of the causes above stated, and have received no greater Bounty than $100 from the United States, **are now entitled to $50 Additional Bounty.**

**Widows or Heirs** are entitled where the soldier died in service or subsequent to discharge prior to July 28, 1866, by reason of wounds or disease contracted in service.

**Heirship for Additional Bounty** is in the following order: 1st. To the widow if not re-married prior to July 28, 1866. 2d. To the children who were minors July 28, 1866. 3d. To the parents jointly, or surviving parent if one is deceased.

**Soldiers** who served at any period for **9 months** or over, and were honorably discharged **for any cause,** and who again enlisted for 3 years and **who received only $302** for last service, can have the records amended to show veteran muster, and **are entitled to $100,** making Veteran Bounty. **Heirs** of such deceased soldiers are entitled to the amount.

**Loss of Discharge** does not debar from Bounty or Pension.

## PENSIONS.

**Wounds, Rupture, Disease, Injuries, or Deafness** contracted in the United States service demand Pension if disability exists, partial or total.

**Pensioners** are entitled to **Increase** if their disability becomes greater; or if dissatisfied with prior examination of Surgeon, an appeal can be taken therefrom, provided satisfactory reasons are shown.

**Widows** are entitled to Pensions if not re-married, provided their husbands died of wounds, injuries or disease contracted in the service; and are allowed for each child under 16 years of age.

**Fathers and Mothers** allowed Pension where dependence can be proved on Son who died of wounds, injuries or disease contracted in the United States service.

**Soldiers** whose names have been dropped from the Pension Roll, can have them restored where the disability warrants such action.

**Patents.** We procure Patents for new inventions, and our advantages in this respect are excelled by none, as we are in close proximity to the Patent Office, and have efficient aid of reliable and extensive experience.

**Commutation of Rations.** All Soldiers or the heirs of those who suffered imprisonment are entitled to receive pay therefor for the full period of confinement.

**Arrears of Pay** and all other claims prosecuted with energy and promptness.

**Attorneys Fees** are regulated by law, and when allowance of a claim is made, Draft is forwarded to the claimant by the Second Auditor of the Treasury. **Fees for Bounty, payable only when claim is allowed.**

Give Post Office address in all cases, and enclose postage stamps for replies with all communications.

Address—Col. Creager Frederick City, Md.

Colonel Luke Tiernan Brien, chief-of-staff to General J. E. B. Stuart, was born in Frederick in 1827. In 1883 Brien and his wife returned to Frederick and purchased a large estate, which they called Tyrone.

Courtesy of the Historical Society of Frederick County.

Authors' Collection

This circular was published after the Civil War by Geo. Bancroft & Co. concerning bounties and pensions. The handwritten note around the margins, signed by Col. Creager of Frederick City, reads as follows:

"A soldiers widow who was such July 28th, 1866, even should she have married again since that date is entitled to the $100. Additional bounty of $100 if she remarried too soon and has a child by the soldier still under 16 years of age the child in most cases is entitled to it. Read this circular carefully and see. All soldiers that are entitled to this bounty additional should apply at once. Read this circular carefully. See your discharge as to where you were enrolled. Please hand this to a discharged soldier or to a soldiers widow or any heir of a dead soldier."

An order was issued to the provost marshal of Frederick calling for the arrest and seizure of property of those residents of Frederick who aided the Confederates in 1864.

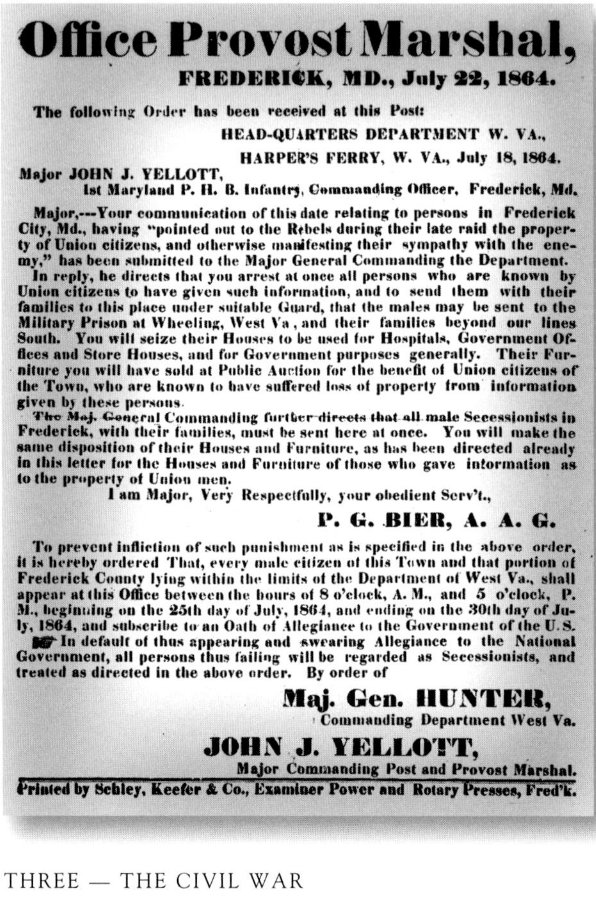

# Office Provost Marshal,

## FREDERICK, MD., July 22, 1864.

The following Order has been received at this Post:

HEAD-QUARTERS DEPARTMENT W. VA.,
HARPER'S FERRY, W. VA., July 18, 1864.

Major JOHN J. YELLOTT,
1st Maryland P. H. B. Infantry, Commanding Officer, Frederick, Md.

Major,—Your communication of this date relating to persons in Frederick City, Md., having "pointed out to the Rebels during their late raid the property of Union citizens, and otherwise manifesting their sympathy with the enemy," has been submitted to the Major General Commanding the Department.

In reply, he directs that you arrest at once all persons who are known by Union citizens to have given such information, and to send them with their families to this place under suitable Guard, that the males may be sent to the Military Prison at Wheeling, West Va., and their families beyond our lines South. You will seize their Houses to be used for Hospitals, Government Offices and Store Houses, and for Government purposes generally. Their Furniture you will have sold at Public Auction for the benefit of Union citizens of the Town, who are known to have suffered loss of property from information given by these persons.

The Maj. General Commanding further directs that all male Secessionists in Frederick, with their families, must be sent here at once. You will make the same disposition of their Houses and Furniture, as has been directed already in this letter for the Houses and Furniture of those who gave information as to the property of Union men.

I am Major, Very Respectfully, your obedient Serv't.,

### P. G. BIER, A. A. G.

To prevent infliction of such punishment as is specified in the above order, it is hereby ordered That, every male citizen of this Town and that portion of Frederick County lying within the limits of the Department of West Va., shall appear at this Office between the hours of 8 o'clock, A. M., and 5 o'clock, P. M., beginning on the 25th day of July, 1864, and ending on the 30th day of July, 1864, and subscribe to an Oath of Allegiance to the Government of the U. S. ☞ In default of thus appearing and swearing Allegiance to the National Government, all persons thus failing will be regarded as Secessionists, and treated as directed in the above order. By order of

### Maj. Gen. HUNTER,
Commanding Department West Va.

### JOHN J. YELLOTT,
Major Commanding Post and Provost Marshal.

Printed by Schley, Keefer & Co., Examiner Power and Rotary Presses, Fred'k.

Courtesy of Fredericktown Bank & Trust

**80**    CHAPTER THREE — THE CIVIL WAR

# ROGER BROOKE TANEY

Roger Brooke Taney was born in Calvert County, Maryland, on March 17, 1777. During his professional career, he was attorney general, secretary of the treasury, and chief justice of the Supreme Court. Taney was married to Ann Key, sister of Francis Scott Key, on January 7,1806, and they had six daughters and a son who died in infancy. Taney moved to Frederick in 1801, where he practiced law until moving to Baltimore in 1823.

A supporter of Andrew Jackson for president in 1824 and later during his successful campaign in 1828, Taney became attorney general and later secretary of the treasury and a trusted advisor in Jackson's administration.

Nominated by Jackson for associate justice of the Supreme Court on January 15, 1835, Taney remained unconfirmed due to political opposition in the Senate. Jackson nominated him again during the next session of Congress, this time to fill the late John Marshall's seat, and, in spite of Whig opposition, Taney was confirmed on March 15, 1836.

Chief Justice Taney is chiefly known for his opinion in the case of Dred Scott vs. Sandford. Taney ruled that since slaves were not citizens, they could not sue in the federal courts. He also asserted that the Missouri Compromise was unconstitutional and that Congress had no right to abolish slavery from the territories. The decision was so controversial that it is considered one of the causes of the Civil War.

Taney died in 1864, a very controversial man. However, his reputation has improved since the Civil War, and he is considered by many to have been one of the great chief justices.

Chief Justice Earl Warren spoke these words at the dedication of the monument at Taney's grave in Frederick in 1954: "In a manner of speaking, today's tribute helps redress an old wrong — helps erase the calumny which Taney's enemies had hurled at him during his lifetime and which superficial historians preserved as gospel truth for a time after his death. Few men in American life — and surely no justice of the Supreme Court — have been so grossly misrepresented as Taney."

*Authors' Collection*

Jacob Byerly

# CHAPTER 4

# THE BYERLY LEGACY

## Three Generations of Photographers

### JACOB BYERLY
Founded Frederick's First Studio in 1842

### J. DAVIS BYERLY
Son, Continued Studio 1868

### CHARLES BYERLY
Grandson, Continued Studio 1899 Until the Studio Collapsed in 1915

# DAGUERREOTYPE

Photography first came to America in 1839 in the form of the daguerreotype, named after Louis Jacques Mandé Daguerre, a French painter who began experimenting with the process as early as 1826. For the next 20 years photography was the laboring process of using silver-coated copper plates that were polished mirror bright; fumed straw yellow and rose red with vapors of iodine, chlorine, and bromine; and exposed in a bulky wooden camera with a "slow" crude lens for several minutes; developed over heated mercury and fixed, gilded, washed, and fitted into small palm-size, velvet-lined hinged cases. The process was crude, yet it produced a sharp "positive" image of subjects, which are relatively permanent and will not fade. The glass-plate negative process was not developed until 1859.

When one considers the laborious task of toting the heavy camera equipment, and working in small ventless darkrooms, and inhaling the noxious and toxic chemicals that were required to develop the daguerreotype, then one can certainly begin to appre-ciate the work and skill of the early daguerreotype photographers.

In 1842 as hundreds of enthusiasts raced to establish themselves as photographers with galleries in cities across the country, Jacob Byerly had already begun establishing a photog-raphy business in Frederick, and a reputation that would extend for over 75 years and three generations of Byerlys.

*Daguerreotype of Jacob Byerly, circa 1842*

Courtesy of Mrs. Frank Kelly

*Daguerreotype of J. Davis Byerly, son of Jacob Byerly. Photographed by Jacob Byerly on July 9, 1869.*

*Courtesy of Mrs. Frank Kelly*

*Hal Byerly as a young woman. Photographed by her father, Jacob Byerly. Daguerreotype, circa 1858.*

*Courtesy of Mrs. Frank Kelly*

*Daguerreotype of a young boy believed to be J. Davis Byerly, son of Jacob Byerly. Photographed by Jacob Byerly, circa 1842.*

*Courtesy of Mrs. Frank Kelly*

*Daguerreotype of Hal and Grace Byerly, sisters of J. Davis Byerly. Photographed by their father, Jacob Byerly, circa 1844.*

*Courtesy of Mrs. Frank Kelly*

Jacob Byerly, considered an early trailblazer in the photographic field, was Frederick's first photographer. His fine work, along with that of his son, John Davis Byerly, and his grandson, Charles Byerly, both of whom inherited his skills and continued the studio he established in Frederick before the Civil War, is the source for many of the vintage photographs from 1842 through 1916 that appear in this book.

A contemporary of Civil War photographer Mathew Brady, history leaves us with little knowledge of Jacob, other than the legacy of his work, which befits someone who spent his life observing and recording the lives of others. What we do know of him comes to us from a maternal family history, *Genealogy of Jacob Bear, 1749-1906.* Jacob was born to Henry and Rebecca Birely (he later changed the spelling to Byerly) on

Feb. 5, 1807, in Newville, Pennsylvania, a small town near Chambersburg.

Originally a teacher, Jacob started his career in photography when he opened his gallery in Frederick in 1842, two years before Mathew Brady opened his New York studio. He made daguerreotypes — a photographic process using silver-coated copper plates treated with iodine vapor — invented several years before by a

*(continued on page 89)*

*Jacob Byerly established his first photography studio in Frederick in 1842 and became one of America's leading pioneers of the daguerreotype method of early photography. Using a large box camera with viewing screen, Byerly produced amazingly sharp pictures, despite the fact that his subjects were required to remain motionless for up to 15-20 minutes.*

Courtesy of Mrs. Frank Kelly

*A severe storm on July 24, 1868, caused Carroll Creek to overflow its banks and devastate downtown Frederick. Jacob Byerly vividly captured the aftermath with a view looking west on West Patrick Street.*

*This portrait of Jacob Byerly, near his retirement in 1868, was likely taken by his son and successor, J. Davis Byerly.*

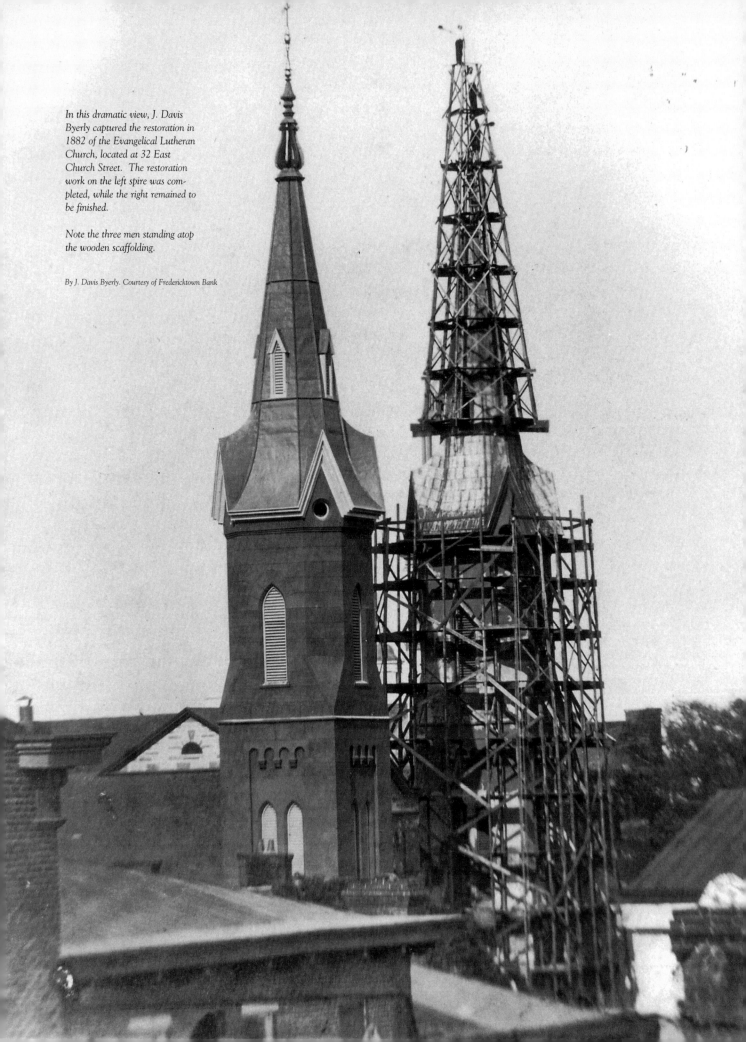

In this dramatic view, J. Davis Byerly captured the restoration in 1882 of the Evangelical Lutheran Church, located at 32 East Church Street. The restoration work on the left spire was completed, while the right remained to be finished.

Note the three men standing atop the wooden scaffolding.

By J. Davis Byerly. Courtesy of Fredericktown Bank

(continued from page 86)

Frenchman, Louis Jacques Mande Daguerre. A Time-Life history entitled *The Camera* hails Byerly as a "trailblazer" in the photographic field, recognizing him as one of America's first daguerreotypists. But Jacob remained on the cutting edge of the technology of his day, switching to the glass-plate technique. Remarkably, at least a thousand glass-plate negatives from the three Byerly photographers have

survived the decades. Jacob produced portraits, slides for the stereopticon (the TV of his time), and cartes de visite, a popular form of calling cards with photographs on them. He sold the business for $2,000 to his son, John Davis, in 1868, but continued to take pictures until his death on March 31, 1885. John Davis Byerly gave us many of the images of the common and the catastrophic events of late Victorian Frederick.

In 1899, the operation passed into the hands of John Davis' son, Charles, where it ended several decades later.

Relatives donated some of the photographers' equipment and props to the Historical Society of Frederick County. The Byerlys' work rests there today, providing a window into our past.

*An 1869 advertising brochure announcing photography services by J. Davis Byerly, successor to his father, Jacob Byerly, from whom he bought the business in 1868 for the sum of $2,000.*

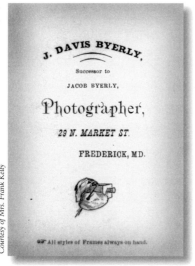

*Courtesy of Mrs. Frank Kelly*

*An 1868 wedding portrait of J. Davis Byerly and Mary Markell, possibly photographed by Jacob Byerly, father of J. Davis Byerly.*

*Courtesy of Mrs. Frank Kelly*

J. Davis Byerly photographed the John Hanshew Markey business and employees in 1884 (right). Located at 7 North Market Street, the business was started in 1858 by O'Neill & Tyler and purchased by J. H. Markey in 1862. The store traded in fashionable hats, high-grade leather boots, shoes, and trunks. Markey died in 1899; however, the business continued well into the early 1900s under the direction of his wife, Mrs. Ida M. Markey.

Court House Square, circa 1875, as photographed by J. Davis Byerly

The cornerstone laying for the Maryland Deaf and Dumb Institute on May 31, 1871 was a gala event that brought many visitors to the site on the grounds of the old Hessian barracks. The ceremonies were conducted by the Masons and were officiated over by H.B. Latrobe of Baltimore, Grand Master of the Free Masons of Maryland. Some of the dignitaries participating in the festivities were members of the Baltimore City Council, Knights Templar of Baltimore, the mayor and aldermen of Frederick, as well as members of the benevolent orders and societies of Frederick and the local fire companies. In 1874, the legislature appropriated an additional $125,000 to complete the buildings.

Note the hand pumper operated by United Fire Company in the left front. This is the first pumper purchased by the department and the only known existing photograph of it.

By J. Davis Byerly. Courtesy of Fredericktown Bank

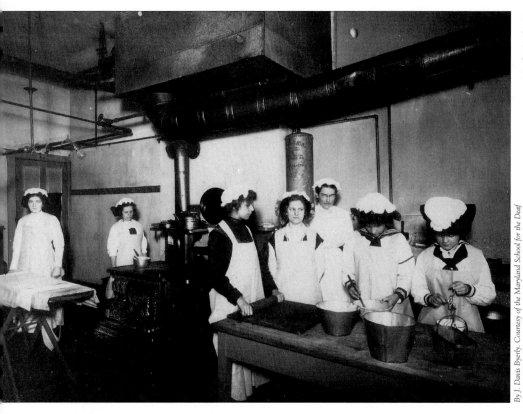

*Circa 1890, home economics classroom of the Maryland School for the Deaf, taken by J. Davis Byerly. The introduction of the electric light better enabled Byerly to photograph his subjects indoors.*

*By J. Davis Byerly. Courtesy of the Maryland School for the Deaf*

*Frederick County National Bank at 1 North Market Street, circa 1892 (right). Note the bank's early iron rail fencing and overhead oil-burning street light.*

*Photographed by J. Davis Byerly. Courtesy of Patsy Moore*

*Maryland School for the Deaf, taken by J. Davis Byerly in 1890. The building with Victorian architectural features was built in 1871. The circular cupola atop the building provided magnificent views of Frederick City until the building was torn down in the early 1960s to enable the school to erect new and more efficient buildings.*

*By J. Davis Byerly. Courtesy of the Maryland School for the Deaf*

In the fall of 1879, the Trinity Chapel steeple was meticulously repaired and repainted for a cost of $535.56. In 1881 the 117-year-old church, located on West Church Street, was demolished and rebuilt for a total cost of $11,067.16. The original steeple and tower were saved, and the new church built around it.

In 1893, the Independent Hose Company of Frederick hosted the state's first Firemen's Convention, at which time the fire company also celebrated its 75th anniversary.

Photograph by J. Davis Byerly
Courtesy of Paul and Rita Gordon

Independence Day Firemen's Parade in 1890, photographed by J. Davis Byerly. The Independent Hose Company was located at 12 West Church Street. The upper floor of the building housed the Odd Fellows Hall, next door was the bowling alley-saloon of Georth Seidling. The large building to the right was the Carlin House, located on the corner of West Church and Court streets. It offered rooms at $1.50 per night. Note: the eagle that adorned the cupola of the firehall was removed and later misplaced. It was recently purchased by an antique collector in Florida, and arrangements have been made for its return to the fire company.

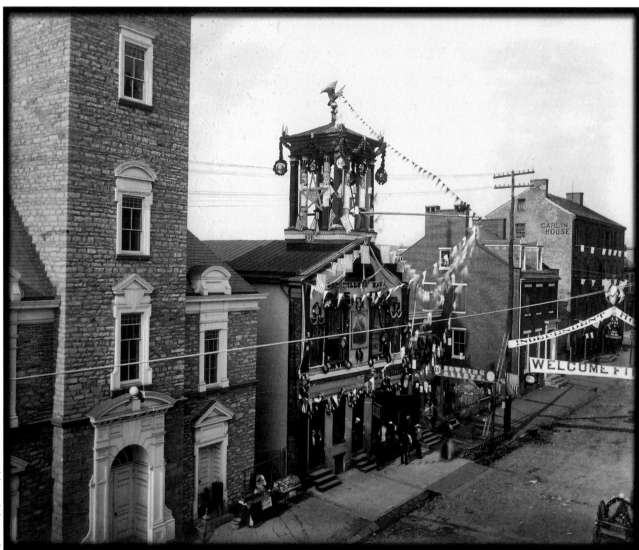

*Church Street sleigh ride, circa 1893. Sebastian G. Cockey, at the reins, pauses for photographer J. Davis Byerly in front of the Methodist Episcopal Church on the first block of East Church Street. Son Sprigg Cockey and daughter Miss Nannie (later Mrs. John Brosius) join Cockey for the winter's day ride. The building later housed a golf shop, owned by Rush Lewis. By the mid-1930s, Lewis turned the property into the Tower Apartments. It is now the site of the city's first parking deck. To the right, at 19 East Church Street, is the building that today houses the Visitor Center and office of the Tourism Council of Frederick County.*

*A gathering at the head-quarters of the Salvation Army at the corner of Bentz and Fourth streets, circa 1894. Note second photographer on right.*

*A portrait of the Byerly and Markell families taken in the courtyard of the Byerly residence at 110 West Patrick Street in 1891. The building was demolished prior to 1980 to make room for the new county courthouse.*

**Left to Right, Front Row:** *Mable Steel and Sophia Kemp (daughters of Stoll and Hallie Markell Detrick), Mary Catherine Chapline (daughter of J. Davis and Mary Markell Byerly), Hally Carter (daughter of James and Annie Walker);*

**Second Row:** *Charles Byerly (son of Charles Byerly and Mary Markell Byerly), Mary Markell Byerly (wife of J. Davis Byerly), Sophia Markell, George Markell, Louis Markell, Annie Walker (daughter of George Markell), John Byerly (son of J. Davis and Mary Markell Byerly);*

**Third Row:** *J. Davis Byerly, Hallie Markell Detrick, Stoll Detrick, Elizabeth Markell (daughter of George Markell), Mae Smith Markell (wife of Louis Markell), James Walker.*

By J. Davis Byerly. Courtesy of Mrs. Frank Kelly

A gathering at the corner of Church and Court streets, circa 1888. The ball pictured is similar to the one rolled from Cumberland to Baltimore in support of William Henry Harrison during his successful bid for the presidency in 1840.

Note the Potts residence prior to the addition of the third story.

By J. Davis Byerly. Courtesy of Mrs. Frank Kelly

Wm. W. Fleming Tobacco, Cigars, Snuff & Company, circa 1894, was located on West Patrick Street next to Frederick County National Bank.

*Humorous studio setting of a young boy playing with fireworks, first of a two-part photographic essay.*

*Note elaborate backdrops and furnishings. Photographed by Charles Byerly, circa 1902.*

*This portrait of a young woman, circa 1903, is a wonderful example of Charles Byerly's talent for studio settings and lighting.*

*A humorous studio setting with father and son, circa 1903, possibly to celebrate the New Year Holiday.*

*Charles Byerly was fond of photographing holiday and festive occasions, such as this Easter setting with mother and daughter, circa 1903.*

*Charles, the third of the Byerly family photographers, became well known for his ability to photograph his subjects in dramatic and interesting settings. Note: the man pictured, circa 1902, is believed to be a photography assistant to Charles Byerly.*

*The young gardener, George Markell Chapline (born April 1900, died 1965), was the grandson of George Markell and J. Davis Byerly. Photographed by (uncle) Charles Byerly, circa 1902.*

*Child shown bandaged up from exploding fireworks by Charles Byerly is part two of a two-part photographic essay.*

By Charles Byerly, Authors' Collection

*J. Davis Byerly photographed the workers during the construction of the stone foundation for the railroad bridge over the Monocacy River at Frederick Junction, circa 1885.*

By J. Davis Byerly, Authors' Collection

*Rooftop view of Trinity Chapel (foreground) and Evangelical Lutheran Church, circa 1900, by Charles Byerly.*

*Stage of City Opera House, circa 1899, by Charles Byerly.*

By Charles Byerly, Courtesy of Patsy Moore

*The shutters remained closed during the day on the lower level of homes along West Patrick Street in an effort to keep out the dust and noise of the early automobile. Circa 1907 by Charles Byerly.*

*C. Thomas Kemp Dry Goods, circa 1907. The building, located on the northeast side of the Square Corner, had just undergone extensive restoration.*

*By Charles Byerly. Authors' Collection*

*The city's first auto mechanic and service center was Solt's Auto Garage, located on East Patrick Street. It was owned by James E. Solt. Circa 1910.*

*Charles Byerly photographed the crowd gathered for the laying of the cornerstone of the YMCA on May 16, 1907.*

Birely's House of Music, corner of Church and Market streets, circa 1902. The city's first musical instrument emporium was started in 1888 by Judge J. M. Birely. Note the barber shop and barber pole next to Trinity Chapel. Photographed by Charles Byerly.

*Photo Courtesy of Authors' Collection*

Frederick trolley car No. 43 travels west on West Patrick Street. The large buildings for the Marken & Bielfeld printing business and the Hotel Frederick can be seen on the right. Circa 1906 by Charles Byerly.

Collapse of the Dutrow's Soda Fountain and third-floor Byerly Studio and building at 29 North Market Street on April 14, 1915. For some unknown reason the front facade and floors of the building collapsed. No injuries were reported, and the building was refurbished in 1916. Charles Byerly, faced with the total loss and destruction of his studio and equipment, ended the business, according to relatives, and never again seriously pursued photography as a commercial venture.

Citizens National Bank

# CHAPTER 5

# 1865-1899

Flood of 1868 Causes Great Damage

School for the Deaf Built

The News Founded by William T. Delaplaine

Many Local Businesses Established

Frederick City Hospital Built

Admiral Winfield Scott Schley Visits Frederick

With the end of the Civil War, soldiers returned to Frederick from both the North and the South. Naturally, citizens who had held differing views harbored ill feelings, and some attempted to force the returning Confederate soldiers to sign an oath of allegiance. Eventually, however, people overcame their differences, and relatives and friends who had fought on opposite sides joined together to rebuild their community.

Local business and industry had been hurt by the war. The area saw few real estate transactions during this period, and almost no buildings were constructed. A large portion of the C&O Canal was badly damaged, as well as telegraph lines and sections of railroad track, including many of the bridges over the Monocacy River. Frederick had to repair the damage as quickly as possible so the town could once again function as Frederick County's center of commerce.

Hardest hit by the war were the farmers. Those whose crops were damaged by Union troops were reimbursed by the federal government; but those who suffered losses at the hands of the Confederacy were not.

Frederick's banks once again came to the rescue by offering loans to get the farmers back on their feet. With its abundance of farmland and its strategic location on established transportation routes, Frederick quickly regained its health and prospered. New industry (continued on page 109)

The first Methodist preacher came to Frederick in 1770 at the invitation of Edward Drumgole. Members worshiped in private homes until they built the first Methodist Episcopal Church on West Church Street in 1792. The membership grew steadily and the building was enlarged in 1806 and 1828. As the membership continued to grow, a lot on East Church Street was purchased in 1841, and a new church was built. That building was torn down and the church shown, circa 1890, was erected in 1865. The church property later was converted into apartments and was torn down to make way for the Municipal Parking Deck. The building to the right is now the Visitor Information Center.

Jacob Byerly captured the destruction
of the July 24, 1868, flood in this view
of South Market Street. More than a
half-million dollars worth of property
was damaged when Carroll Creek
overflowed its banks and flooded
city homes and businesses.

In 1866 the Reverend Osborne Ingle and
his family arrived at All Saints' Parish and
took up residence at 113 Record Street,
formerly the home of Dr. William Tyler.
The parish finally purchased the property
in 1878. Soon after his arrival, Dr. Ingle
officiated at the reinterment of Francis Scott
Key and Mary Lloyd Key in Mount Olivet
Cemetery. Tragedy upon tragedy befell
the Ingles while they resided at Record
Street. On April 5, 1881, their 11-year-old
daughter Bessie died. In January 1882,
five of the Ingle children died in a period of
less than two weeks during the diphtheria
epidemic that raged through the area. The
following year, Mrs. Ingle and their infant
died during childbirth. Dr. Ingle served
the community for 43 years and died on
September 20, 1909.

*A sketch of City Hall, built in 1872 on the site of the market and town hall, built in 1769.*

*On September 13, 1862, the county jail, located on South Street, was destroyed by fire. A new three-story brick jail was constructed from 1875 - 1876 on the same site at a cost of $72,000. In addition to containing cells for prisoners, it also provided accommodations for the sheriff and his family.*

(continued from page 106)
began locating in Frederick, as did insurance companies and financial institutions.

As if the war were not enough to slow Frederick down, it also had to contend with flooding during this period. Throughout its history, Frederick has been flooded several times by Carroll Creek, the small stream flowing through the city, causing considerable damage and loss of property. The most serious flooding in the latter part of the 1800s occurred in July 1868, when the swollen creek overflowed its banks and did more than $500,000 worth of damage. Serious flooding occurred again in 1876 and 1886. During this time, it became the custom to ring the United Fire Company bell to warn citizens of the rise of the creek during and after severe rainstorms.

Many other events of note occurred in the late 1860s. Among them, the Maryland Deaf and Dumb Institution (now the Maryland School for the Deaf) was founded in 1867 adjacent to the site of the Hessian Barracks. The school opened in 1868 with 34 students under the guidance of principal Charles L. Cooke. New buildings for the school were completed in 1874.

In the spring of 1868, the first circus to make a transcontinental tour, Dan Castello's Circus and Menagerie, left Frederick by train and arrived in San Francisco on July 26, 1868.

Louis McMurray came to Frederick to open a canning factory in 1868. Area farmers were, to say the least, skepti-

*Courtesy of Patsy Moore*

*Endorsed by the Medical Association, Montevue Hospital was built in 1870 by the citizens of Frederick on property donated by the Brunner family of Schifferstadt. The citizens wanted to ensure that the insane, poor, sick, and indigent of the area would be treated in a humane way. Rather than build an almshouse, they erected a modern facility to care for those in need. Dr. William Turner Wooten was the first administrator, from 1870 to 1872.*

cal of McMurray's idea and refused to sell him their corn. Undaunted, McMurray purchased land and planted his own corn. His factory was a success. In 1876 he received the highest award for canned corn at the Philadelphia Centennial Exposition. Two years later he was honored in Paris, where he received gold medals for his canned corn and oysters. As a result of McMurray's success, Aaron and Joseph Rosenstock in 1891 established another cannery, the Frederick City Packing Company, in Frederick.

Another successful venture in the late 1800s was the City Market, originally built after Lord Baltimore issued a permit to the city in 1746, and operating in the rear of City Hall in 1873. The weekly market gave residents and county farmers a place to buy and sell cattle, farm produce, and other goods. With the advent of the trolley in the early 1900s, the City Market became extremely successful and remained so until the advent of the automobile and grocery stores made it unprofitable.

Although many Frederick citizens prospered after the Civil War, the development of laborsaving devices for factories put a number of people out of work. Thus, Frederick suffered during the national financial panic from 1873 to 1878.

During this time of hardship, a committee of area residents tried to persuade the federal government to pay back the ransom money demanded by Confederate General Jubal Early when he passed through Frederick in *(continued on page 113)*

*Courtesy of the News Post*

*Some of the employees of Routzahn & Bowers stand on East Patrick Street in 1876. The lumber business was founded in 1868 by Joseph Routzahn and William D. Bowers. Mr. Bowers changed the name to William D. Bowers Lumber Company in 1886 when he acquired full ownership. Upon his death in 1888, his wife and son, Harry, took over the operation. Grayson Bowers joined his brother in 1893. The building was erected in 1868 and the building to its left in 1876. The two buildings were joined in 1891 and an addition was made in 1904. A grist mill was operated on the site until 1896.*

*This 1875 view shows the front and back of the two remaining barracks buildings on South Market Street. The third barracks was razed in 1874 to make room for the north wing of the School for the Deaf.*

*Courtesy of the Historical Society of Frederick County*

Courtesy of the Historical Society of Frederick County

*This woodcut shows Frederick as it looked from the Maryland School for the Deaf in 1878. In addition to Frederick's famous spires, the Montevue Home and many of the tanneries and canning factories can be seen.*

Courtesy of the Historical Society of Frederick County

*Dr. William Baltzell built this home on East Church Street in 1834. In 1879 the home became the Loats Orphans Asylum and was operated as such until 1956. The building is now the home of the Historical Society of Frederick County.*

*Court House Square, circa 1880. In 1818 Colonel John McPherson began installing iron railings manufactured at Catoctin Furnace around the courthouse to prevent animals from roaming on his property. He succeeded in angering many of the townspeople, and the railings were finally removed in 1888. Through the generosity of the public-spirited General James C. Clarke, a public fountain was erected in front of the courthouse after the railing was removed.*

*United Fire Company's pumper, Lily of the Swamp, circa 1890. Built by Clapp & Jones of Philadelphia, the Lily arrived in Frederick on a railroad flatcar on February 20, 1878, and was immediately criticized by the members of rival fire companies. She quickly silenced her detractors. On February 23, a demonstration was held to prove the capability of the pumper. The engine was placed on the corner of Church and Market streets. Pipes were laid and her boiler was fired up. The builder had promised she was capable of propelling two streams of water over the Trinity Tower, and if she failed he would take the engine back to Philadelphia. The Lily succeeded that day, and shortly thereafter broke the record held for many years by the Juniors when she threw a stream of water 274 feet behind Birely's tannery. The Lily served Frederick well for 54 years and was rewarded for her service by being placed on display at the Smithsonian in Washington. Prior to her departure for Washington, numerous ceremonies were held in the city. The Lily of the Swamp participated in one last "fire" when she was towed to the scene of a fire staged in her honor. She was also honored by a parade through the city and a banquet held at the United Fire Company.*

(continued from page 110)

1864 just prior to the Battle of the Monocacy. On June 22, 1874, House of Representatives Report No. 746 of the 43rd Congress stated: "It is not the usage or duty of nations to make compensation to its citizens for damages which they sustain in time of war by the public enemy .... The claim is not one which can justify a departure from the rule of public law on the subject." Regardless of that report, the effort to obtain reimbursement continued until 1986. The interest on the loan far exceeded the original $200,000, and it was not until October 1, 1951, that the city repaid its debt to the banks.

Agricultural fairs were held only occasionally in Frederick County until the late 1800s, but that soon changed. In 1876 the Frederick County Agricultural Society bought a large piece of land on East Patrick Street for its permanent home and the Great Frederick Fair. The first fair was held at the fairgrounds in 1878, and a fair has been held every year since.

The 1880s brought many changes to Frederick. Beginning in 1880 and continuing for several years, Frederick County welcomed a large number of immigrants from several eastern European countries.

Many improvements were made in the city. The cobblestone streets were repaved; the telephone, which met with immediate acceptance, was introduced in 1883; and gas lights were replaced by electric ones in 1887 and 1888.

(continued on page 118)

*Courtesy of the Historical Society of Frederick County*

*The Lampe family stands in front of their store at 203 North Market Street during the summer of 1881. Standing, second from left, is the Reverend William Lampe; Mary Eva Lampe, holding their son, Arthur Christian Lampe; seated on the step is Mrs.Oscar (Grace Rhoads) Lampe.*

# FREDERICK NEWS-POST

William Theodore Delaplaine, above, and his partners Thomas Schley and Victor Marken, produced the first edition of *The News*, a five-column, four-page broadsheet printed on a flatbed press, on October 15, 1883. Mr. Delaplaine would live only 12 more years, but his paper would flourish and survive to the present day. It is one of only a small number of daily newspapers in the country still owned and operated by the descendants of its founder.

William was born to Theodore C. and Hannah Ann Delaplaine on January 3, 1860, at the

*When The News was first published in October 1883, the printing company was located in the upper floors of the Whalen Building at 4, 6, 8, and 10 North Market Street.*

Delaplaine Mill (now known as Michael's Mill) along the Monocacy River in Buckeystown. He received some early schooling there before moving with his family to Frederick in 1875. He studied at the Eastman Business School in Poughkeepsie, New York, graduating with high honors before returning to Frederick in 1880 at the age of 20.

After the Civil War, Frederick's growth stagnated until the 1880s when new industry started in Frederick. William saw the need for a quality printing operation to support area business and established a printing company in 1880 with Marken and Schley. Marken had a reputation as a competent printer and Schley was a businessman who sold his lime manufacturing business to the M. J. Grove Lime Co. Schley was also an uncle of William's future wife, Fannie Birely, and brother of future Frederick Mayor Gilmer Schley. The printing company was known as Schley, Marken and Delaplaine.

The new company was located on South Market Street in the MacGill Building. It prospered and moved to larger quarters at the northwest corner of Patrick and Court streets, and a little later to the upper floors of the Whalen Building at 4, 6, 8, and 10 North Market Street. It was here that the first edition of *The News* was published in October 1883.

Originally, *The News* was a morning publication, but

by January 1884 had become an evening paper. Three rival papers, *The Call* and *The Times* and *Weekly Times*, were purchased and merged with *The News* during this time period. In December 1883 a weekly newspaper was also started by the printing company, which in 1888 switched to semi-weekly. *The Semi-Weekly News*, as it was called, was published until December 1953.

After Marken left the partnership, the company was called Schley and Delaplaine, and then W. T. Delaplaine and Company until 1888. On June 14 of that year, the prospering printing business was incorporated as The Great Southern Printing and Manufacturing Company, with Delaplaine elected as president. The other members of the corporation were Dr. Peter D. Fahrney, vice-president; Charles S. Howard, secretary; Thomas Schley, treasurer; George Birely; Lewis E. Birely; and Lewis A. Rice.

Also in 1888, in need of still more space, the business moved to the second and third floors of The Mutual Insurance Company building at 44 North Market Street, where it printed *The News* until 1917. The first floor was shared by the insurance company in the northern half and John D. Hendrickson's dry goods shop in the southern half. Conditions in the building were not always optimal for its first-floor occupants. The heat from the steam boilers was welcome in winter, but oppressive in summer, and the building would shake every time there was a press run. Since printing is not a clean operation, this, no doubt, was an incessant problem for dry goods merchant Hendrickson.

In July 1890, an agreement was made with the American Press Association guaranteeing that *The News* would receive

*The Schley, Marken and Delaplaine printing company was originally located in what was known as the MacGill Building (white building shown here) on South Market Street in 1880. The building was torn down in 1908 for the rebuilding of Citizens National Bank.*

by telegraph important national and international news items, thus giving its readers the most current news.

From January 1886 to March 1898, the editor of *The News* was Folger McKinsey, who would later be known as the famed "Bentztown Bard," a columnist for the Baltimore *Sun*. He wrote about his experiences in Frederick in his daily column for the Baltimore paper.

In February 1895 a terrible blizzard struck the area, and as always *The News* was on hand to cover the weather story. This story, however, had a tragic ending. William T. Delaplaine, founder of the newspaper, contracted pneumonia while distributing food to the needy and died on February 19, 1895, at the age of 35.

His legacy was carried on by his descendants. Of his four sons, three became presidents of the corporation: Robert E. (1941); William Theodore, Jr. (1955); and George Birely, Sr. (1964). The fourth son, Edward Schley, became a Maryland State Court of Appeals judge and would forever after be known as "Judge" Delaplaine. George Birely Delaplaine, Jr., is the current president, and his sons, James W. and John P., are also active in the business. Frances Ann Delaplaine Randall, granddaughter of the founder, is a director and the newspaper historian. Her son, George E. Randall, is vice president and general manager.

One other item from the paper's early history should be noted: In 1916, the Great Southern Printing and Manufacturing Company bought out a rival daily newspaper, *The Frederick Post*, which had been in existence since 1910. *The Post* was published from a building on North Court Street. Because the two publications ran many of the same ads and features, common items were transferred between the two locations. After about a year and a half of workers pushing a heavy handcart of lead type up and down Church Street, the

*Folger McKinsey, who became known as the "Bentztown Bard," was the editor of* The News *from 1886 to 1898.*

*Post* building was purchased in September 1917 and used to print both papers. They have been known since as *The Frederick News-Post*, with *The News* continuing as an afternoon edition and *The Frederick Post* remaining a morning paper.

The two publications continue the tradition established by the founder by bringing not only local, national, and international news to the citizens of Frederick, but a sense of community as well.

*The News was published from the second and third floors of this building at 44 North Market Street from 1888 to 1917, at which time its printing operations were merged with that of* The Frederick Post *and moved to North Court Street.*

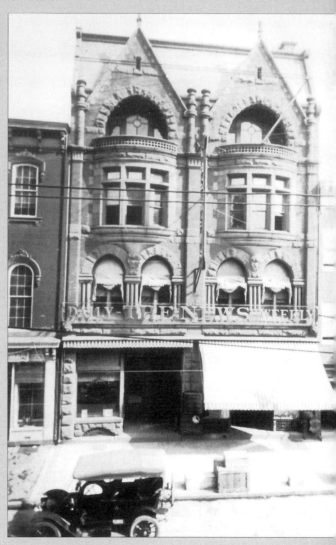

Photos Courtesy of the News-Post

Citizens National Bank, circa 1890, was located on the corner of South Market and East Patrick streets. Chartered January 2, 1886, the bank quickly established itself in the community. The original directors of the bank were: Louis McMurray, James McSherry, George William Smith, O. J. Keller, D. H. Hargett, John S. Ramsburg, William G. Baker, D. E. Kefauver, C. M. Thomas, M. N. Rohrback, James A. Elder, and Joseph D. Baker. These citizens of Frederick were men who possessed sound judgment combined with astute business skills. Citizens, as a member of the national bank system, was the first local bank to introduce the policy of paying interest on savings accounts. Due to the bank's growth and need for additional space, the building was torn down and a new one built in 1908.

Staff members and patients enjoy the fresh air on the steps of the Montevue Hospital, circa 1885.

Frederick County National Bank, located on the northwest corner of Market and Patrick streets, circa 1885. It was founded as Frederick County Bank in January 1818 with a charter granted by the General Assembly and began operations in June 1818. In 1865, it became Frederick County National Bank. The first president was John Grahame, and the first cashier was George Baer. The members of its first board of directors were Roger Brooke Taney, John Grahame, John P. Thompson, Abraham Shriver, Frederick Schley, John Schley, John L. Harding, Stephen Steiner, Lewis Creager, Christian Kemp, Henry Steiner, and William Goldsborough.

(continued from page 113)

From October 1881 until the spring of 1882 Frederick suffered an epidemic of diphtheria in which 315 people died. The disease was to return several more times in the next few years, prompting a strict cleanup of waste in the community and penalties for violators. Many businesses were believed responsible for the diphtheria epidemic, among them the canning factories, slaughter shops, tanneries, and hog pens, not to mention the cesspools and privies of private homes. The Maryland General Assembly created a Department of Health in 1886, making each county responsible for enforcement of the regulations. The city appointed a committee and took measures to correct the situation as quickly as possible.

Frederick produced a hero during the Spanish-American War in 1898. Commodore Winfield Scott Schley, a Fredericktonian and a graduate of the United States Naval Academy in Annapolis, led three battleships and a cruiser into the harbor of Santiago, Cuba, allowing American troops to storm and capture San Juan Hill. When the Spaniards tried to escape from the bottled-up harbor, their ships were destroyed. Because of his success, the hero of Santiago, Commodore Schley, was promoted to the rank of admiral for "conspicuous conduct in battle." ☆

Courtesy of the Historical Society of Frederick County

*The second city reservoir was under construction in the 1890s (above) and was located at the site of the present Kehne Memorial Park on West Seventh Street. The reservoir was completed in 1895 at a cost of $35,000, providing a capacity of 8 million gallons. The completed city reservoir, circa 1905 (right), displayed a figurine and showering fountain.*

# CITY RESERVOIR

In 1825 a meeting was held at Talbott's Hotel to organize a water company. Some of the citizens involved with this enterprise were Gideon Bantz, Stephen Steiner, William Tyler, and John McPherson. Stock was sold and the company brought water through wooden pipes from an artesian well 2½ miles northwest of the city to a reservoir. This supply proved inadequate, however, and the project was abandoned before 1840. In 1839 the town government was given permission by the legislature to raise $75,000 by means of a lottery. The town borrowed $30,000 in 1844 and $8,000 in 1845. Construction was begun in 1844 and was completed on November 22, 1845, at a cost of $90,000.

Courtesy of Stanley Sandersgill

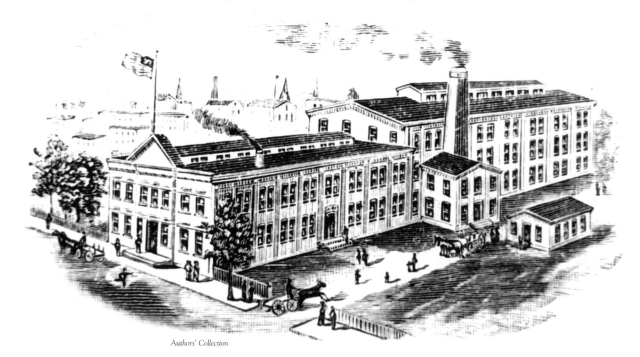

*Authors' Collection*

In 1887, a group of area businessmen founded the Frederick Seamless Hosiery Company located at the corner of East Patrick and North Wisner streets under the management of John L. Johnson. Begun with ten knitting machines, the business was intended to give young ladies in the area a dignified way to earn their livelihood in clean and congenial surroundings. The knitting mill prospered and within two years merged with the Union Manufacturing Co., maintaining the original directors, David Lowenstein, M. E. Getzendanner, Jno. Baumgardner, George H. Zimmerman, and Thomas H. Haller. The company manufactured only the highest quality of men's, women's, and children's hosiery. It also had embroidery machines and its own dyeing and printing facilities.

C.E. Cline's Carpets & Furniture business was established in 1888 and occupied 10,000 square feet on South Market Street. Mr. Cline was a native of Frederick and in addition to operating the furniture business, was also president of the Crystal Plate Ice Company. Through the years he served as president of the Commercial State Bank and was a director of the Mutual Insurance Company and Citizens National Bank.

*Courtesy of Karl Zimmerman*

E.C. Houck's Park Stables at 69 West Patrick Street, 1889. Mr. Houck, a native of Frederick, took great care of the animals entrusted to him. In addition to boarding horses, he provided local citizens with the best vehicles available for hire. He also bought and sold all types of horses to suit the needs of his customers.

P.L. Hargett & Co., circa 1888. Located on South Market Street, it was considered to be the leading hardware store in the city. Operated by four brothers, the store covered 10,000 square feet and carried every imaginable hardware item. Two large warehouses stored farm equipment and other bulky goods.

S. MARKET ST., FREDERICK, MD. 66

*D.F. Davis Coach Factory (above and at right), 1889. Located at 89-91 South Market Street, it was the oldest coach factory in the city, having been established in the early 1800s. Mr. Davis purchased the business from Mr. D.A. Castle about 1885. The factory's primary business was the design and manufacture of buggies and wagons to the customer's specifications. In addition, it provided quality repairs to all types of conveyances.*

*A circa 1890 photo of the Central National Bank at the corner of Church and Court streets. The bank was located here for more than 100 years and for a time rented space to the postal service. Upon Central National Bank's acquisition of First National Bank of Frederick in 1909, the building was sold to People's Fire Insurance Company and the board of directors voted to construct a four-story brick building on the corner of Market and Church streets.*

*Students of Frederick College, March 1889. Seated front row, left to right: H. Ebert, C. Kemp, D. Steiner, W. Saunders, W. Benner, W. Dansberger, C. Byerly, T. Turner. Second row: A. T. Webster, W. Zimmerman, Professor of Mathematics E. C. Shepherd, and C. Groff.*

*Appearances notwithstanding, this is not the scene of a public trial or hanging, but the wedding of Ella Graser and Jacob Kanode. The ceremony was performed by Dr. Edmund R. Eschbach of the Evangelical Reformed Church on October 16, 1890, at the Frederick Fairgrounds.*

*Unknown members of a wedding party descend the steps of the Evangelical Reformed Church, 1890.*

*The Excelsior Sanitary Dairy, circa 1892, located at 207-209 East Seventh Street, is now owned and operated by Dairy Maid.*

# THE MARYLAND SCHOOL FOR THE DEAF

The original Victorian-style building for the Maryland School for the Deaf (above) was removed in the 1960s to allow the school to replace it with modern and serviceable buildings to meet the educational needs of the students. The Maryland Deaf and Dumb Institute was established by an act of the state legislature in 1867. The first meeting of the board of visitors was held on October 3, 1867. The site chosen to build the school was on the grounds of the old Hessian barracks. The state legislature contributed an initial $25,000 and $5,000 annually. Principal Charles L. Cooke opened the school in 1868 with 34 students, some transferring from the Columbian Institution in Washington. In 1870, the legislature appropriated $100,000 for new buildings. The cornerstone laying was held on May 31, 1871. In 1874, the legislature appropriated an additional $125,000 to complete the buildings.

As is obvious from the following photographs, the students who were fortunate enough to attend the Maryland School for the Deaf received a well-rounded education. In addition to learning skills that would allow them to support themselves, they also participated in activities that stimulated them intellectually and physically.

**Circa 1890, photographs by J. Davis Byerly.**

Photos Courtesy of Maryland School for the Deaf

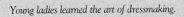

*Young ladies learned the art of dressmaking.*

Maryland School for the Deaf students learned not only proper serving techniques, but also received instruction in etiquette.

Male students received instruction in various trades, such as printing, carpentry, and boot making.

A classroom at the Maryland School for the Deaf.

Courtesy of Patsy Moore

*A parade viewed from West Patrick Street, near the area where the Weinberg Center is today, circa 1890. The building behind the large tree on the left side is Frederick County National Bank. Dr. Thomas's Drug Store was across the street on the corner of North Market and East Patrick.*

*Members of the Frederick Bicycle Club, circa 1890.*

Authors' Collection

*A parade coming down
North Market Street,
circa 1890.*

Courtesy of Patsy Moore

*Martin N. Rohrback's grocery store at
7 West Patrick Street, next to the City
Hotel. The hotel was built in the early
part of the 19th century by a stock company that included Henry Clay as a member.
General Lafayette occupied room 16 when
he was feted here in 1824. Frederick's
farmers and area businessmen found it to
be a congenial place to conduct business
and to relax over dinner or join friends for
a drink or a game of billiards.*

Authors' Collection

Courtesy of Paul and Rita Gordon

*Citizens National Bank, at the southeast
intersection of Patrick and Market streets,
circa 1890.*

This is a photograph, circa 1890, of the first demonstration of electric light in Frederick. The photograph was taken by J. Davis Byerly (with the help of his assistant J. Fred Kreh - on table) at the 42 North Market Street office of The News. Williamson's Drug Store, established in 1869 next door to The News, was the first business to convert to electricity. From left to right are Dr. J.A. Williamson, druggist; Charles S. Howard, business manager of The News; George Hane of Washington, D.C.; Dr. P.D. Fahrney; William T. Delaplaine, publisher; Jacob B. Tyson, fertilizer manufacturer; James A. Brown, bookkeeper; unidentified man; Folger McKinsey, editor of The News.

Built in the 1890s, this house at Seventh and Market streets was the home of Union Army Captain Joseph Groff and his wife, Susan Smith Groff. The building served for many years as the home of radio station WFMD. After a stormy battle to preserve it in 1973, the building was demolished in order to construct a medical complex; however, the new facility was not erected, and the site remains a parking lot.

The Palmetto Brush Company was established in 1890 at the site of the Page Foundry on West South Street. In the early 1900s, the name was changed to Ox Fibre Brush Company and the business was relocated to a 12-acre site on East Church Street. In addition to the factory, the plant included a sawmill and warehouse. The machinery used was patented by Ox Fibre Vice President McClintock Young. The company manufactured many grades of vegetable fiber brushes that were sold worldwide. Goodwill Industries is now housed in the buildings.

City Opera House, Freder

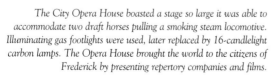

City Opera House
Frederick Md.

The City Opera House boasted a stage so large it was able to accommodate two draft horses pulling a smoking steam locomotive. Illuminating gas footlights were used, later replaced by 16-candlelight carbon lamps. The Opera House brought the world to the citizens of Frederick by presenting repertory companies and films.

*Courtesy of Patsy Moore*

*View looking up North Market Street from atop a building on West Church Street, circa 1891.*

*Courtesy of Charles Watson*

The Montrose Iron Works was organized in 1897 by the Diven Brothers, who built a small steel and machine shop at the corner of East Seventh Street and the tracks of the Pennsylvania Railroad. In 1905 the plant was leased to Barber & Ross and later to John Mitchell, Jr., who operated the company under the name Frederick Iron Works. In 1910, Mitchell combined with Elmer P. Morris and the company was reestablished under the name of Morris Iron Company, at which time the factory was greatly enlarged. In 1913, the company was again enlarged and it became known as the Morris Iron and Steel Company. A steel casting plant was installed, and the plant had the melting capacity of 40 tons of iron and 10 tons of finished steel castings per day. A 20- by 50-foot casting room occupied the rear of the building, and the second floor was devoted to pattern work. A two-ton hydraulic elevator and a five-ton traveling crane were installed in the casting room to move the heavy castings. During the fall of 1913, the company produced 250 printing and engraving presses for the Bureau of Engraving and Printing, Washington, D.C. Now known as Frederick Iron & Steel, the company remains a vital part of the Frederick community.

South Market Street looking south from the United Fire Company, circa 1893. The arch was erected in celebration of the 1893 Firemen's Convention. A saloon on the northwest corner of West All Saints Street was owned by Scott S. Welty and featured Tannhauer Beer. Jacob A. Kidwiler owned a saloon on the southwest corner.

Pioneer Livery Stables, circa 1893. The business was owned by Edward Sinn and was located on the northwest bank of Carroll Creek at 47-49 South Market Street.

The 1893 Firemen's Convention parade on Market Street featured this horse-drawn hose carriage, which was the first to be purchased by Independent Hose Company.

Junior Fire Company No. 2 was all decked out for the first Firemen's Convention in 1893. At the time this picture was taken, the fire company was located next to Farmers and Mechanics Bank on North Market Street. The Opera House and City Hall are to the right of the fire company. The Junior Fire Company was organized in 1838, and the engine house on Market Street was built in 1846. The first steamer in Frederick was purchased by the Juniors in 1876, and in 1877 they purchased Frederick's first hook and ladder. The Junior Fire Company is now located at 524 North Market Street.

*Mountain City Mill (right center), circa 1895, was located next to the B&O Railroad depot. Owned by D. W. Deitrick of Philadelphia, the mill produced 400 barrels of flour a day. At present the building is being renovated and serves the community as the Delaplaine Visual Arts Center.*

*Birely's House of Music on the corner of Church and Market streets, circa 1902, was the city's first musical instrument emporium. It was started in 1888 by Judge J.M. Birely. Note the piano crates, barber shop, and "barber pole" next to Trinity Chapel. Photographed by Charles Byerly.*

*This photograph by J. Davis Byerly captures not only the fashion of the late 1890s but also the mood of his subject.*

CHAPTER FIVE — 1865-1899   **135**

The city of Frederick, circa 1896, looking southeast in this view from Trinity Chapel. In the foreground is the first block of North Market Street, with (left to right) the Hendrickson Building, which housed The News; J.A. Williamson Druggist at 30 North Market Street, which sold prescription drugs worldwide; Neidig & Miller, with the second floor used by the International order of the Redmen; the Walker & Bennett building at 26 North Market; and Fredericktown Savings Institution.

The circus comes to town, circa 1895.
Animals and entertainers arrived by train
and paraded with great fanfare down
Patrick Street, eventually arriving at the
Frederick Fairgrounds.

A parade was held in 1896 to celebrate the opening of Boys' High
School. The driver of the team pulling the replica of the schoolhouse
is Harry B. Wetter. His children used the model as a playhouse for
many years. Prior to 1896, the North Market Street school was
used to educate elementary school boys; high school boys studied in
a different building, at 314 North Market Street. In 1912 the high
school was moved to a new building on Elm Street, and the North
Market Street school became an elementary school once again. It
has been in continuous use since it was built in 1878. It housed the
first classes of Frederick Community College, and for a time was the
home of the Frederick County Extension Service and the audio-
visual department of the C. Burr Artz Library. In November 1970
the Frederick County commissioners granted permission for the
building to be used as a senior citizens' center.

# FRANCIS SCOTT KEY MONUMENT
*Dedication - August 9, 1898, Mount Olivet Cemetery*

*Courtesy of the Historical Society of Frederick County*

*Some of the descendants of Francis Scott Key who participated
in the dedication ceremonies of the monument.*

## KEY

*A Poem By "The Bentztown Bard,"
Folger McKinsey*

He gave us the song of the banner,
He pictured its symbol in light
Of the glory that marks it forever
When freemen contend for their right.
He named it and flamed it with splendor
As he gazed from the prow of his ship,
And the star-spangled banner still echoes
On every true patriot's lip.

He gave it a new birth of beauty,
He lifted it for us so high
That the soul of its faith and its freedom
Shall nevermore weaken and die.
He loved every fold of its colors,
He worshipped the thing that it meant
To the soldier who serves in the battle
Or sleeps on his arms in the tent.

He gave us the spell of its meaning,
He showed us its heart and its soul
To abide in their wonder forever
Through all the great ages that roll.
He gave it a voice and a legend,
He gave it a purpose and will
That stir in the heart of the nation
And echo in ocean and rill.

He gave us the song of the banner,
He gave us the hymn of its might;
He lit it with melody's splendor,
He made it an anthem of right.
And it grows with the growth of the nation,
It lives and it shines and is true
To the gospel of faith and of freedom -
Our flag of the Red, White and Blue.

Aerial view of the city in 1895 taken from the cupola atop the Maryland School for the Deaf.

Admiral and Mrs. Winfield Scott Schley visited friends and family in Frederick in 1899, soon after the end of the Spanish-American War.

Winfield Scott Schley was born at Richfield, once the home of Governor and Mrs. Thomas Johnson. He was named in honor of his father's close friend, Mexican War hero General Winfield Scott. A graduate of the United States Naval Academy in 1860, Schley saw a great deal of foreign service during his navy career. He is most well known for the events that occurred in the harbor at Santiago, Cuba, in July 1898. Temporarily in charge of the U.S. fleet at the time, Schley ordered the destruction of the Spanish fleet when it attempted to escape. Supreme Commander Admiral Sampson, 20 miles away at the time, criticized Schley and tried to claim credit for the victory. Schley endeared himself to the American people when he said, "There is enough glory for all." He was promoted to Rear Admiral in 1899 and retired October 9, 1901. He was buried at Arlington National Cemetery on October 2, 1909.

*More than 30 inches of snow fell between February 3 and February 17, 1899. The temperature dropped as low as -4 degrees.*

*Near the end of the 19th century, two very lucky children celebrated Christmas with their own ceiling-high trees decorated with elaborate Victorian dolls and soldiers.*

*Looking down on Court House Square from Trinity Chapel, circa 1899.*

Courtesy of Paul and Rita Gordon

Laying of Trolley Tracks

# CHAPTER 6

## 1900-1949

Trolleys Become Established as Mode of Transportation

Hood College Built

Calvary Methodist Church Built

Bentz Street Widened

Baker Park Opened

Francis Scott Key Monument Re-Dedicated

In 1900 Frederick was hometown USA: a quiet tree-lined community with active churches and civic clubs.

Many industries attempted to move to Frederick County, but met with little encouragement. The descendants of the founding families wanted Frederick to retain its atmosphere as a prosperous but quiet community. Growth, however, was necessary. Farmers needed an improved transportation system to get their produce to market in Baltimore, and young people needed jobs. Growth through the early part of the century was steady, but slow. In 1914 the population was about 14,000.

During World War I most men from Frederick fought in Company A, 115th Infantry of the 29th Division. The 29th was also known as the Blue and Gray Division because it contained both southern and northern units. The 115th Infantry fought with courage against the Germans in the Alsace Sector and during the Meuse-Argonne offensive, which effectively crippled the Germans. Twenty-five percent of the 115th Infantry's 3,834 men were either killed, wounded, gassed, or missing during the war.

After the war, Frederick had little to offer in the way of attractive jobs, so many young people left. At the

(continued on page 151)

*Courtesy of the Historical Society of Frederick County*

*This building at 110 North Court Street, circa 1900, has served as a law office for many years and is currently the home of a real estate office. Its most well-known tenant was Roger Brooke Taney, who practiced law in Frederick from 1801 to 1823.*

*Western Union Telegraph Company, circa 1900. Western Union purchased the B&O telegraph lines from the railroad in 1887. The telegraph office was located on North Market Street next to Dutrow's Confectioner at 29 North Market Street. Dutrow's was located in the same building as the Byerly studio and the Selective Service office. Note the delivery bicycles in front.*

*Employees of Birely's Palace of Music deliver a piano in the early 1900s. The business was founded by J. M. Birely in 1888 at the corner of North Market and West Church streets. Mr. Birely sold pianos, organs and other musical instruments, as well as classical and popular sheet music. Repairs were made in the rear of the shop. Mr. Birely was elected to serve as a judge of the Orphan's Court in 1903.*

*The northeast corner of North Market and East Patrick streets, circa 1904. The building shown in the center of the picture is Kemp's Dry Goods Store before the third story was added and the building was remodeled.*

*The Masonic Temple on West Church Street was built by Columbia Lodge No. 58 and Lynch Lodge No. 163, Ancient Free and Accepted Masons, and was dedicated on December 12, 1902. Freemasonry flourished in the area from the time of the American Revolution. The United States Post Office was located in the building until the completion of the new building on East Patrick Street in 1917.*

(continued from page 148)

onset of the war, Frederick County had been an important grain-producing area. After the war, over-production caused many farmers to go out of business. Overall, though, the county was able to maintain its agricultural base and made the transition to dairy farming.

The Great Depression hit hard in Frederick County, just as in the rest of the country. Because of its lack of industry, Frederick took longer to recover than many areas of the country. Again, young people left to find better job opportunities.

With the Japanese attack on Pearl Harbor during World War II, many local men enlisted and served in all the services, in both the European and Asian theaters. During the Normandy invasion, Company A, 115th Regiment was among the first units to land.

Area men who did not participate in the fighting helped out by working in shipyards and aircraft plants in Baltimore. Local women aided the Red Cross by packaging bandages. As in other areas, items in short supply, such as gasoline and sugar, were rationed.

One important development during the war had far-reaching effects on Frederick County's future economic growth. Hundreds of men and women were assigned to Camp Detrick to take part in biological warfare research. These included

(continued on page 156)

Looking toward stage in City Opera House during United Fire Company BAZAAR held in 1905 to raise money for purchase of the Company's horses.

Looking toward entrance of the City Opera House during fund-raising BAZAAR of United Fire Company in 1905. The proceeds bought first and only horses.

*A circa 1900 display of United Fire Company equipment at the Opera House. The items featured in the two photographs were used during the first Firemen's Convention held in Frederick in 1893.*

*Photos courtesy of United Fire Company*

Authors' Collection

# TROLLEY

In 1830, the citizens of Frederick turned down the opportunity to become a main-line stop on the Baltimore & Ohio Railroad. As a result, the railroad located Frederick Junction about two miles south of the city. Frederick became one of the first cities to have rail service and the first to have a branch line. When the Western Maryland Railway built its Baltimore-Hagerstown line in 1870, Frederick was bypassed again and the line ran 17 miles north of the city through Mechanicstown (Thurmont). In 1872, Frederick became a branch line of the Pennsylvania Railroad.

The farmers and citizens of Middletown and its environs were forced to use the National Pike to carry their goods by wagon to market either in Frederick or Hagerstown. The road was in very poor condition and had some extremely steep grades. Several attempts were made to bring railroad transportation from the Middletown area to Frederick. A group attempted to form the Metropolitan Railroad from Washington, DC, to Hagerstown in 1853, but the effort failed due to a combination of investor apathy and the interference of Baltimore businessmen who felt threatened by loss of business. In 1884, the Frederick & Middletown Railroad foundered when it raised only 10 percent of the funds necessary.

Finally, in April 1893, George W. Smith, a wealthy farmer and

*A crowd watches as trolley tracks are laid on North Market Street in 1905. Oscar B. Coblentz stands on the tracks with his back to the photographer, and Charles Esworthy holds a crowbar. Among those standing to the right are Ernest Pettingall, George M. Hett, Jacob Rosenstock, "Pots" Shouman, and Joseph Houff. On the curb at right are: Dr. J. R. Radcliff and Charles M. Gilpin. At left are Benjamin Rosenour and leaning on his bicycle, Paul Kennedy. The life-size horse at right is the trademark of Castle Harness Shop.*

property owner, organized a group of local investors who formed the Frederick & Middletown Passenger Railroad. After additional consideration, they reincorporated in 1894 as the Frederick & Middletown Railway with a new charter allowing the company to carry freight as well as passengers. The citizens of Middletown and the surrounding area were enthusiastic about the improved mode of transportation, but Frederick's citizens reacted the way they had when they turned away the main line of the Baltimore & Ohio Railroad. Most felt that it would encourage industry, attract an undesirable element, and disrupt the quiet and beauty of Frederick. In May 1893 the *Frederick Examiner* chastised its readers: "Soon we shall likely have a score of Electric Roads binding our towns and villages together, and our grand old country will enter upon a career of progress never dreamed of by slow-going fogies, and the doubts and cavils of skeptics will vanish like mists before the morning sun."

All funding for the railroad was obtained locally, property was purchased for the right-of-way in 1895, and construction was started in the spring of 1896. The railway line began at the corner of Carroll and Patrick

streets and headed west. The trolleys were operated by electricity and were powered by a pole on top of the car that was connected to an overhead electric cable. Due to its limited budget, the company was forced to purchase power from the Frederick Light & Power Co. The first rolling stock consisted of three cars, two double-truck open summer cars, and a closed combine nicknamed "Old Mike" that could carry freight or passengers. By August, track was completed over the five-and-one-half miles from Frederick to

Braddock Heights, offering rural residents practical and inexpensive transportation as well as a means of getting their goods to market quickly. In addition to the scenic ride, passengers were thrilled on the steep grades and sharp turns. After several trials, full operations were ready to begin, and on Sunday, August 23, 1896, thousands of Frederick's citizens rode the trolleys to the park at Braddock Heights. After a day of excitement, Railway President George Smith and 109 people boarded car number 10 for the return trip to Frederick. The

*A 1911 photo shows Frederick & Middletown Railway trolley 31 as it makes the turn from North Market Street onto East Patrick Street. The Frederick Railroad purchased trolleys 31 and 32 from the J.G. Brill Company in 1910 to replace the steam locomotives on the Frederick-Thurmont line.*

*The Frederick & Middletown Railway terminal on the corner of East Patrick and Carroll streets in 1911. In 1896, the railroad erected a wooden car barn at Carroll and Patrick streets. The shoddily constructed building was razed in 1910 and a new barn was built on Patrick Street. The two-story terminal handled passengers, freight, and express shipments and contained company offices. The track that allowed passengers to board the train inside the building was later removed during expansion and renovation of the building. When railroad service ended, the building was used by Potomac Edison. Today the building is the headquarters of The Frederick News-Post.*

car had a maximum capacity of 48 people. About halfway down the mountain, motorman William Mantz lost control. The trolley picked up speed, shot across a trestle, and left the track when it could not negotiate a curve and crashed into a field. Many of the passengers were seriously injured and one woman was killed. As a result of the accident, the company instituted strict maintenance and safety regulations.

Track laying continued, and on October 21 trolleys began making the nine-mile trip to Middletown. To provide transportation to the fairgrounds, the Frederick City Suburban Railway was organized and construction was completed on October 12, 1896, in time to carry 15,000 passengers to the fair. The company was later merged into the Frederick & Middletown Railway. The car barn was built in November 1896 and the power generating plant was built in 1897. In 1898 trolley service was extended five miles north to Myersville and was incorporated as the Myersville & Catoctin

Railway. In 1902 the Hagerstown Railway opened a line to Boonsboro, coming within eight miles of Myersville, and in December 1904 the Boonsboro line was extended to Myersville. In 1905 the Frederick & Middletown company was taken over by a group of Baltimore businessmen who planned to convert the rail system into a fast electric line to Baltimore, and in 1906 it became

*A photo of the Frederick & Middletown Railway car barn on East Patrick Street, circa 1920. The new car barn was built in 1911 to replace the old wooden one at Patrick and Carroll streets. The Frederick office of Potomac Edison is now located on the site of the car barn.*

*Trolley 172 is shown as it crosses over the Pennsylvania Railroad tracks at the intersection of East Patrick and East streets, circa 1930. Car 172 was purchased from the J.G. Brill Company in 1921 and had a capacity of 48 passengers. It was used to make the last run to Thurmont in 1954. The large building behind the trolley is the Everedy Company and to the right is Sanitary Laundry.*

| Jan. | Feb. | Mar. | Apr. | May | June | July | Aug. | Sept. | Oct. | Nov. | Dec. | Even Hr. | 15 aftr | 30 aftr | 45 aftr |
|---|---|---|---|---|---|---|---|---|---|---|---|---|---|---|---|

**THE HAGERSTOWN & FREDERICK RAILWAY**

Form T-1     TRANSFER     01294

Good subject to the rules of this company for one ride this day over such lines as indicated by punch marks only when presented by person to whom issued, on first car leaving Public Square or Junction of 5th and Market Street, after time punched.

Passengers must examine transfers to see that route and time are properly punched.

Void if offered after time limit expires as shown by punch marks.

*Jg. Moore*
DEPT. OF TRANSPORTATION

*Courtesy of Potomac Edison Company*
*GLOBE TICKET COMPANY PHILA., PA.*

S. MARKET | N. MARKET | W. FIFTH | E. FIFTH | W. PATRICK | E. PATRICK | W. SOUTH | E. SOUTH | EMERGENCY | From | TO

*A transfer issued by The Hagerstown & Frederick Railway in 1920. The ticket reads: "Good subject to the rules of this company for one ride this day over such lines as indicated by punch marks only when presented by person to whom issued, on first car leaving Public Square or Junction of 5th and Market Street, after time punched. Passengers must examine transfers to see that route and time are properly punched. Void if offered after time limit expires as shown by punch marks."*

the Baltimore Frederick & Hagerstown Railway. Their plans died on the drawing board and trolley service continued.

In 1908 a line opened from Frederick to Thurmont, and in 1913 Frederick & Middletown Railway acquired the Hagerstown Railway and renamed the company the Hagerstown & Frederick Railway.

From a group of small, locally-owned electric trolley lines and power plants, the Hagerstown & Frederick Railway would grow to become the Potomac Edison Company.

While in operation, the trolley carried millions of people, tons of freight, locally grown produce, mail, newspapers, and ice. The cars were open in summer and heated by wood stoves in winter, traveling at about 20 miles an hour.

The trolley's inevitable demise was speeded by the introduction of Henry Ford's $500 Model-T in 1908. By the 1920s, Potomac Edison was expanding beyond utilities and trolley operations. The Blue Ridge Transportation Company, owned and operated by Potomac Edison, could travel the same route more quickly and more profitably than the trolley. Passengers riding the trolley to Hagerstown dropped from 3.8 million in 1920 to 500,000 by 1940. Due to a decline in passengers, the trolleys stopped running in Frederick in 1937. World

War II gave the trolleys a brief reprieve, when they were used to haul salvaged material from Jefferson Street to Camp Detrick. When the last trolley made its final trip to Thurmont in 1954, trolley buffs from New York and Ohio mingled with the large crowds of Frederick citizens who bid farewell to an old friend.

*Courtesy of the Historical Society of Frederick County*

*Decorated with a banner, trolley 172 makes one of its four "last" trips from Frederick to Thurmont on February 20,1954. Shown at the controls is R. Dave Smith, president of the Hagerstown & Frederick Railroad, supervised by motorman Morris Remsburg. Blue Ridge Transportation Company buses replaced the trolleys, but were discontinued after a year and a half. In 1955 Potomac Edison removed the electric lines and converted to diesel trains for the freight service to Thurmont. In 1958 the track between Fort Detrick and Thurmont was removed and the only service remaining was that provided to the industrial concerns along East Street. Potomac Edison closed down all operations on April 26, 1961.*

*(continued from page 151)*

military personnel, as well as scientists. Their work continued after the war, and many of them remained in Frederick County, stimulating economic development that continues to this day.

Unlike returning soldiers from World War I, WWII veterans found job opportunities bright. Some went to work at Camp Detrick; others found employment with the new industries locating in the area. ☆

A general hardware and agricultural supplier established in 1869 by B.F. Stewart and J.E. Price occupied this building, circa 1910. This building constructed in 1865, at South Market and West Patrick streets was a most historic site. In 1750 Mrs. Charlton kept a tavern on this site and the County Court held its sessions in the upper chambers. On November 23, 1765, the 12 judges had Court Clerk Darnell and the sheriff arrested for disobeying their stamp paper mandate.

The Arlington Hotel, circa 1903, was located on the third block of North Market Street. The site served as a hotel since the early 1800's. In 1852 it was Derr's Hotel and 1864 the Groff House. In 1920 the Croghan family purchased and restored the hotel, changing the name to the Hotel Frederick. In 1972 it was sold to the city and torn down to make way for a parking lot for Carmack's Grocery.

Walker & Bennett, 26 North Market Street, circa 1904. Originally established in 1877 at 6 West Patrick Street by James Walker, the shop became known as Walker & Bennett in 1904 when Mr. Bennett was made Mr. Walker's partner after 25 years of service. In addition to his responsibilities as a merchant, Mr. Walker was also president of Frederick Telephone & Telegraph Company and served as a director of Citizens National Bank, the Frederick County Fire Insurance Company, and the Frederick County Agricultural Society. Fredericktown Savings Institution is located to the right of the shop.

*Courtesy of Patsy Moore*

*Jug Bridge, circa 1905. In 1804, a turnpike was begun from Baltimore to Frederick to aid local farmers in transporting their goods to market. Frederick County resident Leonard Harbaugh, considered one of the best stonemasons of his time, was commissioned for $55,000 to build the necessary stone bridge across the Monocacy River. After the bridge was completed, he built a large demijohn next to the bridge. On March 3, 1942, the bridge collapsed, dropping some 20 feet of the structure into the river. The "jug" is now located off Bowman Road, near Interstate 70. The large house to the left at the top of the hill was built in 1894 and was at one time the home of Samuel Rosenstock, benefactor of Hood College and namesake of Rosenstock Hall. The white house to the right of the road was a toll house and tavern.*

Courtesy of Farmers and Mechanics National Bank

*For a time, banks were allowed to print and issue currency. This ten-dollar bill, dated May 25, 1905, was issued by Farmers and Mechanics National Bank.*

# FREDERICK CITY HOSPITAL

Frederick City Hospital was organized in 1897 and chartered in 1898. Miss Emma J. Smith donated seven acres opposite Park Avenue for the hospital. Contributions were solicited and many fund-raising activities were conducted, including plays, lawn fetes, and bake sales.

On July 11, 1901, the Masons of Lynch Lodge 163 marched behind the United Fire Company Drum and Bugle Corps for the laying of the cornerstone. The $8,353 contract was awarded to Michael Gittinger for the construction of the two-story brick building. The City Hospital was formally opened on May 1, 1902, and contained 16 private rooms and three wards for men, women, and children. Privileges were extended to all city and county physicians. The

*An ambulance waits in front of Frederick City Hospital, circa 1906. Note the newly completed south wing, donated by Margaret Hood.*

hospital's first class of nursing students (Edna Gilpin, Mrs. Gertrude Hamilton Kussmaul, and Mrs. Bertha Stewart Wright) graduated in 1904. The last class of nine students graduated in 1968.

Through the generosity of Margaret S. Hood, the Hood Wing was added to the south side of the hospital in 1905 and the James Mifflin Hood Wing was added to the north side in 1907. X-ray equipment was installed in the basement in 1912. Mrs. Georgianna Houck Simmons donated funds for the establishment of a nurses' home, which was completed in 1913. In 1914 a maternity ward and clinical lab were opened and in 1916 a baby ward was established.

In 1929, the Baker-Shank Annex and the Johnson Memorial wing were opened. The Baker wing contained rooms for children, maternity, and colored patients (prior to 1929, colored patients were treated at a small hospital on

West All Saints Street). The Shank wing contained a new dining room, private and semi-private rooms, and new operating rooms.

On May 12, 1952, the hospital's name was officially changed from Frederick City Hospital to Frederick Memorial Hospital.

Frederick Memorial Hospital has grown with the needs of the community. In the 1950s, the North Wing and the Gambrill Wing opened. In the late 1960s, the three-story Y wing was built. During the 1990s, a state-of-the art emergency room and a parking deck were added. Records indicate that in 1904, 138 patients were treated at the Frederick City Hospital. Frederick Memorial Hospital treats 40,000 patients annually, with privileges extended to more than 200 physicians. The hospital's Regional Cancer Therapy Center is rated one of the finest in the United States.

*Courtesy of Frederick Memorial Hospital*

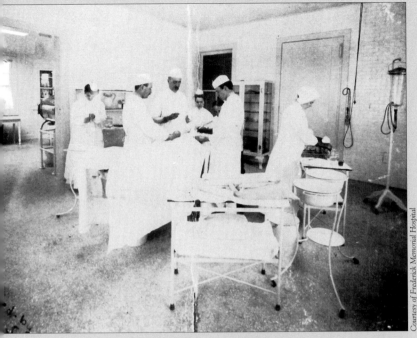

Surgery at Frederick
City Hospital, circa
1908.

A 1926 view of
Frederick City
Hospital. Note
the addition of the
third floor.

James Mifflin Hood, husband
of Margaret Scholl Hood, was
born in Baltimore in 1821
and died in 1894. Mrs. Hood
donated funds for the building
of the second Hood Wing at
Frederick Memorial Hospital,
and the cornerstone of the
James Mifflin Hood Memorial
Wing of Frederick City
Hospital was laid on
November 2, 1906.

A private room in
the Hood Wing of
Frederick City Hos-
pital, circa 1908.
The charge for a
private room in the
early 1900s was $8
to $25 per day.
Five "free" beds
were available for
worthy cases.

*Myers Livery Stable, circa 1906, was located in Locust Alley (now Maxwell Avenue) between East Third and East Second streets. George Edward Myers purchased the business from Horace C. Zacharias in 1901 and operated it until 1909. The young lady pictured is Mary Elizabeth Stewart Myers, nicknamed "Lizzie," granddaughter of the owner.*

*Junior driver William B. Davis, engineer George E. Buesing, and fireman William H. Shipley outside the firehouse on North Market Street, circa 1906.*

*Students of Girls' High School march in a parade on North Market Street, just passing Church Street, circa 1908.*

Courtesy of the Historical Society of Frederick County

Courtesy of Stanley Sandergill

*Employees of Obenderfer & Son Undertaking, circa 1906. Note the display of Victorian wicker in the window and the large gas lamp hanging in the entrance. The business was established by Mr. L .Obenderfer in 1840; his son, F.W. Obenderfer, became a partner in 1885. They originally specialized in furniture, including antiques, and later operated as a funeral home.*

*Employees of the Montrose Iron & Steel Company standing in front of two large core drying ovens, circa 1908. The employees (left to right) are Mr. Kuttmar, Bill Noggle, Tom Heart, Scooner Mull, Fred Sheeley, and John Blumenour.*

Courtesy of Stanley Sandergill

*Rockwell Terrace, located in the northwestern part of the city, circa 1908. The plots were laid out by Frank C. Norwood and recorded on May 8, 1905. It was named for Elihu Hall Rockwell, who formerly owned most of the land. Mr. Rockwell was born in New England in 1790. Upon reaching manhood, he moved to Frederick County, where he became a prominent educator. He spent his last years in Frederick, and after his death, his home at the head of West Third Street was removed to open the street. Other land for Rockwell Terrace came from the Evangelical Reformed Church and the estate of Lewis H. Dill.*

*A photo of the remains of the Mountain City Mill on South Carroll Street shortly after it was destroyed by fire in 1906. At the time of the fire, it was operated as a flour mill. In the 1850s, the building was used as a whiskey rectifying house. This was the second time a fire had destroyed a building on this site. The original stone building was destroyed by fire in 1893. The Great Southern Printing and Manufacturing Co. purchased the building, rebuilt it, and used it for storage of huge rolls of paper used to print the Frederick News and Post. Scorch marks can be seen to this day on the exterior north wall. The building is now the home of the Delaplaine Visual Arts Center. In the distance can be seen the Visitation Academy, the Church of Saint John the Evangelist, Evangelical Lutheran Church, and the Evangelical Reformed Church. The Frederick County Farmer's Exchange is at the lower left. Photographed by Charles Byerly.*

*South Market Street looking south from the Square Corner, circa 1908. A Monon Steam Laundry wagon is making a delivery in front of Citizens National Bank and M. L. Etchison Furniture and Undertaking on the left. C.E. Cline Carpet & Furniture is on the right, as well as Monon Steam Laundry at 42 South Market Street. Landis Jewelry, founded in 1893 at 23 South Market Street, still operates at that location.*

*West Patrick Street looking east, circa 1908. The people on the left are standing in front of the Marken & Bielfeld printing office. The building was later torn down to make way for the Frederick Motor Company.*

*West Patrick Street looking west toward the old stone tavern, circa 1908. West Patrick Street to Telegraph (now Jefferson Street) was known as "Bentztown." The area from Telegraph west was called "Battletown."*

# GREAT FREDERICK FAIR

Frederick County's first agricultural society was formed on November 3, 1820. The first exhibition was called a cattle show and fair and was held May 23 and 24, 1822, at George Creager's Tavern, two miles east of the city (this was the second fair ever held in the state). Fairs were held annually for several years and then stopped. A farmers' club was formed on November 20, 1849, to revive local interest in agriculture and to educate area farmers about the careful use of fertilizers. The group changed its name to the Frederick County Agricultural Society in May 1853 and incorporated in June 1854. Because the Hessian barracks lot was fenced, it was chosen as the site of the group's

first fair October 12 - 14, 1853, and the fair was held there annually until 1860. During the fair, the east wing of the barracks was used to display domestic fabrications and farm machinery. In 1859 the Maryland State Fair was held in conjunction with the Frederick Fair, and the society leased five acres of land near the barracks for the event. The fairs were suspended during the Civil War and did not resume until 1867. In 1867 the Agricultural Society sold 139 life memberships in the society to raise money to purchase land for a new fairgrounds. This became necessary when the state legislature chose the Hessian barracks property as the site for the Maryland School for the Deaf. In September 1867 the

group purchased 14 acres of land in the eastern suburbs of the city from General Edward Shriver and several more acres from William Falconer. Additional land was purchased in 1875, bringing the size of the fairgrounds to 33 acres. The half-mile race track was used for the first time in 1871. During the 1870s President U.S. Grant, Horace Greeley, and President Rutherford B. Hayes attended the fair.

*Citizens from far and wide line up outside the entrance to the fairgrounds on East Patrick Street, circa 1910.*

ENTRANCE TO "FAIR" GROUNDS, FREDERICK, MD.

*Authors' collection*

A crowd gathers to enter the sideshow exhibit, circa 1908. It was promoted as a "Trained Wild Animal Arena. Greatest Exhibition Of Its Kind In The World. Do Not Be Misled."

The participation of area children has always been an important part of the fair. Here, children prepare to demonstrate their various equestrian skills, circa 1910.

Well-dressed fairgoers stroll along the midway at the "Great Frederick Fair" in 1910. Attractions in the grandstand that year included high-wire performers, the Sisters Macarte; a troupe of contortionists, the Demonella Trio; and "World-Famed Gymnast," Ouda.

Authors' collection

W. PATRICK ST., LOOKING EAST, FREDERICK, MD.    84.

*A view of West
Patrick Street from
Steiner Hill and the
Old Stone Tavern,
looking east toward
Market Street,
circa 1902.*

Authors' Collection

EAST PATRICK ST., FREDERICK, MD.    225

*East Patrick Street from the Square Corner,
circa 1908. Citizens National Bank on the
right is now a branch location of Farmers
and Mechanics National Bank.*

*Courtesy of Patsy Moore*

*The Square Corner at the intersection of North Market and West Patrick streets, circa 1906. From left to right are the Casino Restaurant, Frank's Cafe, Fleming's Tobacco and Snuff Co., Frederick County National Bank, Main's Drug Store, and Markey's Shoe Store.*

*Home of The Busy Corner Bookstore (left), circa 1904. This corner of North Market and Second streets is now the home of Connie's. Capello's grocery store, located across the street, sold fresh fruits and vegetables on open sidewalk displays. Nicole's Deli is now located on this site.*

*Authors' Collection*

*Market Street looking north from the Square Corner, circa 1908. This picture was taken shortly after the third floor was added and extensive restoration work was completed on C.E. Kemp's store (right).*

N. MARKET ST., LOOKING SOUTH FROM SECOND ST., FREDERICK, MD.    232

*North Market Street from Second Street looking south, circa 1904. Farmers and Mechanics National Bank (left) is on the corner, followed by Junior Fire Co., Old Empire Theater (note the placard announcing Moulin Rouge Girls, Big Burlesque Co. "Tonight"), Sappington's Grocery, and the City Opera House.*

*North Market Street, circa 1904, looking north at the site of the City Opera House (right). Walker & Bennett is on the left. Note the wooden barber pole (left) and large rooftop sign, "Use Challenge Flour."*

*Authors' Collection*

*Looking south from the intersection of North Market and Church streets, circa 1904. Kemp Hall (left) held the offices for Frederick Gas & Electric Co.*

*Authors' Collection*

*East Patrick Street looking west, circa 1904. The C&P Telephone building is on the right. Note the three oversized "coffee pots" on a pole (center) that served as a sign for The Frederick Stove Company.*

*This view of North Market Street looking north, circa 1904, shows the Gothic exterior of the Fredericktown Bank and Trust building (right) whose headquarters are still located at this site. Neidig & Miller and the International Order of Redmen were next door. Note the two hanging clocks (left) that advertised Landis Jewelry.*

*The intersection of Court and West Church streets looking east, circa 1908. The YMCA building is on the far right. The Post Office and Masonic Temple were located in the next building, followed by the Independent Hose Company and Trinity Chapel. Note that the cobblestone street was in the process of being bricked.*

*Organized in 1888, the Young Men's Christian Association (YMCA) met in a small room in the Etchison building on South Market Street and in the former parsonage of the Evangelical Reformed Church for many years. A sum in excess of $60,000 was raised by the citizens of Frederick to construct the YMCA's new home on the former site of the Park Hotel on the corner of West Church and Court streets. A widely attended reception was held on New Year's Day, 1908, to show off the building. On the first floor was a cafe that served moderately priced meals. There were reading rooms supplied with daily papers and periodicals. Games such as checkers, chess, pool, and billiards were available. The building contained two regulation-size bowling alleys, a swimming pool, indoor track, and a gymnasium with all the latest body-building apparatus. The third floor contained 22 living rooms for young men, with eight private bathrooms and one general bathroom. The second floor of the building was devoted to offices for members of the association, classrooms, and an auditorium that seated 200 people. Female members were allowed the use of the recreational facilities one day a week. The YMCA had an annual budget of about $9,000.*

This bridge marks the site of the original Barbara Fritchie home on West Patrick Street, circa 1906. The building for Burck & Keefer Plumbing and Tinners (left) was later torn down to widen Carroll Creek. A reproduction of the Fritchie house now sits on this site.

West Patrick Street looking east from Court Street, circa 1904. The New City Hotel and Buffalo Hotel are on the left (now the site of Colonial Jewelry). Note the sign advertising "Smoke The F.K.S. Plantation; The Best Cigar on Earth; 5 cents." The two men with the cart (right) worked for the Frederick Electric Light Company.

*Dill Avenue, circa 1904, looking west from West Fourth Street. Traveling east to west, the street connects Fourth Street with Rosemont Avenue on the way to Yellow Springs. Quinn AME Church can be seen on right of picture. Note: The tracks running the length of the street are part of the WF&G steam route, abandoned in 1910.*

*West Fourth Street (below), circa 1904, looking east toward Market Street. The cannon, projecting from the sidewalk on the left side of the photo, was placed there some time after it was last fired. When James K. Polk defeated Henry Clay in the 1844 presidential election, a man by the name of Duvall fired the cannon from its location at the top of Carroll Street (now known as "Cannon Hill"). Mr. Duvall filled the barrel with clay to signify that candidate Clay had been blown up. Unfortunately, Mr. Duvall was killed when the cannon exploded. The remains of the cannon were later moved from Fourth Street and are on display in the Hessian Barracks.*

*Clarke Place, circa 1908. Located in the southern part of Frederick, across from the Hessian Barracks and the Maryland School for the Deaf, the street was named in honor of James C. Clarke as a tribute to his life-long concern for Frederick's welfare. The land was originally part of a farm owned by Dr. Bradley Tyler. The property was later owned by Harry Bowers, who built the first house in 1894 after the plots were laid out by John F. Ramsburg. The sign (inset) was placed at the locked entrance to the private road.*

*Looking northwest over the rooftops from the bell tower of St. John's, circa 1909. Frederick City Hospital is visible in the upper left of the picture.*

*C.W. Martz and his wife delivering milk to the citizens of Frederick, circa 1905. Milk was delivered early in the morning and cost 7 cents a quart or 4 cents a pint. In winter the cream froze and came out of the top of the bottle.*

# BLACK COMMUNITY

West All Saints Street has been the center of the black community farther back than anyone can remember. The community was once on the edge of the city, surrounded by forest. Blacks began residing in the area of All Saints Street by the mid-19th century. One of the first residents was a slave named John Jenkins, who bought his freedom and purchased land on South Bentz Street. In 1857 he raised the sum of $250, which he paid to slaveholder Francis Sappington to free his wife, Lucy, and their children.

When slavery ended, white residents wanted to keep the blacks close by, because they were employed as servants. Some lived uptown in the areas of Fifth and Sixth streets as well as Klinehart's Alley. A few lived on North Bentz, Seventh Street, Middle Alley, and Maxwell Alley. Most, however, lived downtown on West All Saints Street, South Bentz Street, Ice Street, Court Street, Phebus Avenue, and Broadway as well as sections of East Street and East Church Street.

Although the black residents were allowed to shop for clothing and necessities, they were not allowed to try them on in the stores; they could purchase food, but were not allowed to eat inside. As a result, many shops were opened and home-cooked meals were available from restaurants and canteens or from stands set up along West All Saints Street by its industrious residents. The members of the black community found everything they needed here – grocery and clothing stores, barber and beauty shops, restaurants, churches, schools, civic and social clubs, doctors, dentists, and a hospital. There were even several pubs. On the weekends, blacks from the surrounding countryside traveled to West All Saints Street to shop, pray, and socialize.

*Courtesy of Dr. Blanche Bourne*

*In 1919 Dr. Ulysses Bourne (above) and Dr. Charles Brooks founded the first black hospital in Frederick at 173 West All Saints Street. The hospital operated until 1929, at which time black patients were admitted to a ward in the Baker Wing at Frederick City Hospital. The building is now the home of the Mountain City Elks.*

*Due to segregation, Frederick's black community formed its own troop of the Boy Scouts of America on June 14, 1920.*

*Authors' Collection*

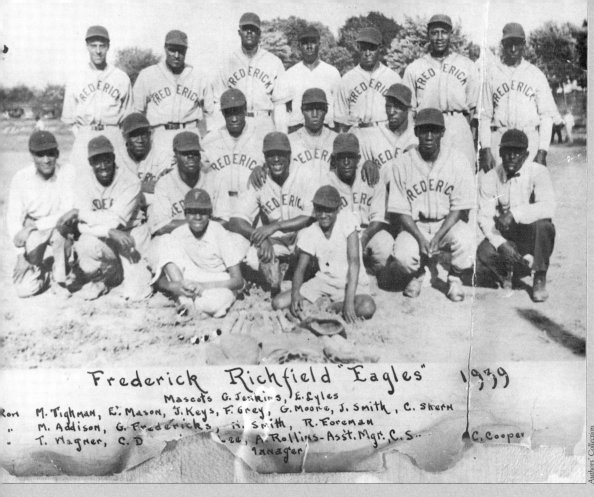

Members of Frederick's 1939 Richfield Eagles, a semi-professional baseball team that played in the black league.

Frederick Richfield "Eagles" 1939

Mascots G. Jenkins, E. Lyles

Row M. Tighman, E. Mason, J. Keys, F. Grey, G. Moore, J. Smith, C. Stern

" M. Addison, G. Fredericks, H. Smith, R. Foreman

" T. Wagner, C. D........ .....ee, A. Rollins-Asst. Mgr. C.S.. C. Cooper
Manager

On October 13, 1937, a kindergarten was founded to meet the needs of the black families in Frederick. Classes were held in the Pythian Castle at 110 West All Saints Street until 1946, when the school was moved to the recreation room of the Lincoln Apartments. In 1949, the kindergarten was named in honor of Esther E. Grinage (right), who had taught the area's black elementary school students for 35 years. With the assistance of Zonta of Frederick, the association became the first black organization to become a member of the Community Chest. When Mrs. Marguerite Quinn, a member of Zonta and strong supporter of kindergarten education, died, she made the association the residual beneficiary of her will. Her bequest was to be used for a building fund; however, in 1973 the Frederick County Board of Education approved public kindergarten in all schools. Mrs. Quinn's endowment was invested, and a scholarship fund was established in 1975 in the name of Esther Grinage. Approximately 200 area students have received grants from the scholarship since it was established. On July 31, 1993, a reunion of students who attended the Grinage Kindergarten was held in the Gambrill State Park Tearoom.

Asbury United Methodist Church, circa 1918. In 1818 the property was the site of a white Episcopal congregation, but by 1864, it had become the home of a black congregation. The church, located on West All Saints and Court streets, was completed in 1921.

The first black high school was built on West All Saints Street in 1921. At that time, black children who attended high school were bused to the All Saints Street school.

An early photo of All Saints Street, circa 1903, clearly
shows the professional businesses that were part of life in
the black community. One of the businesses was run by
William Doley, an ex-slave who set up a blacksmith shop.

Courtesy of the Bourne family

The Park Hotel on the southeast corner of
Church and Court streets was erected in
1850. It was first known as the Eagle Hotel.
It has at times been known as the Dill House
and the Carlin House and in 1908, after
feverish construction, became the home of
the Young Men's Christian Association.

United Fire Company member Basil
Schwearing guides "Dud" and "Doc."
Firemen George Moberly, John Frazier,
and Grayson Haller stand alongside,
circa 1907.

UNITED No. 3, FREDERICK, MD.

90-1

Independent Hose Company put the East's first automobile fire engine into service in the fall of 1909. The gentleman on the left in the white coat is George Wallace. Behind the wheel is William Fleischman, and to his right is James Brust. The man holding the nozzle is Frank Brookey, and the men standing on the rear of the engine (left to right) are: G. Allen Kline, William Heim, and Vernon Derr.

Frederick's first motorized funeral coach was owned by C.C. Carty Funeral Home.

Frederick's first champion Tri-City League baseball team in 1909. The team played at Agricultural Park site of the Frederick Fairgrounds. Later the team turned professional, calling themselves the Frederick Hustlers and included team member Harry Grove, namesake of the Class A Frederick Keys stadium. Top row, second from the right, is Richard F. Nallin, who later umpired in the famous Chicago Black Sox series played in 1919. Nallin owned the farm now a part of Fort Detrick property.

FREDERICK'S CHAMPION BALL TEAM '09

*The first block of West Patrick Street looking back toward the Square Corner, circa 1910. The Buffalo Hotel (left) was owned by Professor Louis Otte, a German immigrant who became widely known for his fine food.*

Authors' Collection

Courtesy of Karl Zimmerman, Sr.

*The Monumental Saloon, circa 1910. This establishment at 102-104 West Patrick Street was owned by Robert A. Farley. It was originally established by Charles Miller and was sold to Charles "Tish" Cramer in 1898. To the far left can be seen the bridge over Carroll Creek. Note that Bentz Street does not yet cross Patrick Street.*

Courtesy of Karl Zimmerman, Sr.

*Interior of the Monumental Saloon, circa 1910. The gentleman behind the bar is Robert Farley and the boy is Franklin "Shorty" Weddle.*

Courtesy of the Historical Society of Frederick County

*United's engine parked in front of the City Hotel on West Patrick Street, circa 1910. To the right is Besant's grocery store.*

# HOOD COLLEGE

Hiram Winchester arrived in Frederick in 1830 and founded a girls' school on North Market Street. In 1845 it was renamed the Frederick Female Seminary, at which time the school received its state charter and credentials. The first catalog was issued in 1846. Classes were conducted in a building (shown at right) still named for the founder (Winchester Hall) on East Church Street. In 1893 the school was renamed "The Women's College." In 1913, Margaret S. Hood donated 45 acres of land in the northwest section of the city near the hospital for the erection of a modern college. In addition to the land, she left a generous endowment. In appreciation of her generosity, officials of the college renamed the school Hood College.

*Authors' Collection*

*Winchester Hall, circa 1898.*

*Courtesy of Robert McCutcheon*

*The horse-drawn carriage for the Women's College, circa 1906, was used to shuttle the students on field trips and daily excursions.*

*Courtesy of Hood College*

*Chemistry class, circa 1905. Students conduct experiments in the well-equipped laboratory.*

President Joseph Apple and his son, Joseph Jr., break ground for Alumnae Hall on the campus of Hood College, April 2, 1914. Prior to the groundbreaking, ceremonies were held in the College Hall. Dr. Apple took great pleasure in the groundbreaking, as he had labored more than 20 years for the expansion of the school.

Margaret S. Hood, benefactress of Hood College. Mrs. Hood also donated two wings to the Frederick City Hospital. The south wing donated in 1905 was named in her honor and the north wing, donated in 1906, was named in honor of her late husband, James Mifflin Hood.

An artist's rendering of Hood College before it was built on Rosemont Avenue, circa 1910.

Alumnae Hall, Hood College, circa 1945.

*A circa 1910 photo of the Female High School. The school was founded in 1896, at which time classes were held in the old rectory of St. John's Church on East Church Street. Due to the building's age and poor condition, it was demolished in 1906 and a new building was put up on the site at a cost of $30,000. The building currently houses some staff members of the Frederick County Board of Education.*

ARMY AIRSHIP, READY FOR FLIGHT TO WASHINGTON, CAMP ORDWAY N.G.D.C., AUG. 21 1911, FREDERICK, MARYLAND.

*On August 21, 1911, one of the first aircraft designed for the army by Wilbur Wright flew from Camp (now Fort) Myer, Virginia, to Frederick, landing somewhere in the area of where Fort Detrick is located today.*

*The White Cross Milk Company, circa 1911. Construction began on the new plant in 1909, located at the east end of town along the B&O Railroad tracks. Employing 25 men, milk production grew to more than 2,700 gallons each day. Refrigerated train cars carried the milk throughout the eastern states.*

*Courtesy of Stanley Sundergill*

*Authors' Collection*

*Students of Frederick College in 1911. Built in 1796, the school, known locally as the Academy, was opened on October 2, 1797, with Samuel Knox as its first principal. The third floor was added in 1877. Frederick College received its charter in 1830. During the Civil War it was used as a hospital. In 1936 the building was razed in order to widen Record Street and construct the C. Burr Artz Library. Among the students pictured are: Clarence Shepherd, D. Chester Kemp, Charles Houck, William Roth, John Byerly, Casper Cline, Albert Ritchie, M. G. Urner, Jr., Richard Ross, William Zimmerman, Charles C. Carty, Harry Shouman, Allen Rohrback, Thomas Van Fossen, Madison Nelson, Milton Lowenstein, Robert Kunkle, Arthur Gambrill, William Markell, Charles Ely, Harry D. Baumgardner, George Wilcoxon, and William Carty.*

*Ideal Garage, circa 1911. Founded in the early 1900s by Elias B. Ramsburg, Sr., the garage originally represented many different automobile manufacturers. In 1909 Mr. Ramsburg entered into a contract with Buick to sell its vehicles exclusively. The corporation was chartered in 1911, and in 1924 it acquired the former tannery property on Carroll Street and expanded the business to 40,000 square feet. In addition to sales of new and used cars, it also provided full maintenance and parts service, operated a machine shop, vulcanized tires, and provided 24-hour, 365-day-a-year storage service. New and used autos were displayed in the second-floor showroom. After Ideal built a new facility at Evergreen Point, the building remained vacant until 1987, when it was converted into a large antiques retail facility.*

*Boys' High School students march up Market Street during the "Safe and Sane" 4th of July parade in 1912.*

*The newly completed Mountain City Lodge No. 29 of the Knights of Pythias on Court Street in 1912. The lodge was chartered in 1869 and at its height of popularity had close to 2,800 members. A small group of members continue to honor its traditions.*

*Courtesy of Carl Brown*

*Courtesy of Stanley Sundergill*

In 1913, Harry L. Ebert sent a postcard to a friend in Lutherville, identifying this shop as the place he worked.

*Barbara and John Fritchie were removed from their original resting places in the Reformed Church Graveyard and reinterred in a stone vault at Mount Olivet Cemetery on May 30, 1913. The elaborate ceremonies were conducted by the members of the Barbara Fritchie Memorial Association. The footstones of the new graves are their original grave markers. On September 9, 1914, ceremonies were held at the cemetery to unveil a monument honoring Barbara Fritchie. It is 13 feet tall and is made of Maryland Guilford Granite on which her name is cut in rounded five-inch letters. The seal of the Barbara Fritchie Memorial Association is designed on a bronze medallion above a tablet bearing John Greenleaf Whittier's poem.*

*The Diehl Memorial Fountain was located at the corner of Church and Court streets, in front of the Law Building (which housed the post office for a time). The brass fountain stood 18 feet high and was erected at a cost of $500. The fountain was named in honor of Marie Diehl for her work in organizing the Frederick Chapter of the Society for the Prevention of Cruelty to Animals. The society started its drive for the memorial in 1909, and the fountain was unveiled on August 17, 1911. The fountain was unique in that it served to refresh both man and beast. In the right rear of the photo is the Post Publishing Co., which began operation on December 10, 1910. The building to the left and behind the fountain is the Frederick YMCA. The fountain was severely damaged when it was hit by a truck, and the top portion of the fountain was salvaged and is now located at the Steiner House.*

*Postcards like this one, printed by M & B Printing, circa 1913, were sold to raise money for the proposed monument to Barbara Fritchie to be built at the corner of North Market and Seventh streets. Due to a lack of funds raised, however, a memorial on a much smaller scale was dedicated in 1914.*

The Maryland National Guard Armory, once home of Company A, 115th Infantry, was built on the corner of West Second and Bentz streets in 1914. When a new armory was built, this building was acquired by the city and is currently used as a day-care center and adult recreational facility.

Escorted by policemen and a drum corps, "Uncle Joe" Walling set off on another of his transcontinental trips on April 1, 1915. Joe Walling joined the United Fire Company in Frederick at the age of 16 and served as a volunteer fireman until his death at the age of 91. He earned his living as a wagon train guide, Indian fighter, cowboy, telephone lineman, soldier, and sailor. He is best remembered locally for his incredible wanderlust, making at least five transcontinental journeys. He financed his trips by selling postcards of himself posing in costumes depicting his various occupations. On the back of one of the cards was printed: "After two unsuccessful attempts to make the Coast on horse and back, both times being injured, I am now walking from Baltimore, Md., to San Francisco, Cal., solely as an endurance test. I am making my expenses by the sale of these cards. Anything you give will be appreciated." Uncle Joe maintained close contact with relatives in Frederick over the years, and after he died in Baltimore on July 2, 1944, he was buried in Mount Olivet Cemetery.

The Frederick Fruit Supply on the northwest corner of West All Saints and South Market streets, circa 1915, was one of several such establishments owned and operated by the three Marino brothers. Anthony Marino is standing by the pole; the boy in the back wearing knickers is Roy Mealey; the young man on the right is Ellwood Brown; and the gentleman standing behind the little girls was known as "Mr. Phil." By using canopies, the establishment was able to expand the size of the shop by placing goods on the sidewalk, protected from the elements. Note the coal-fired peanut roaster in the left foreground. It would be next to impossible to pass up fresh fruit and roasted peanuts!

In 1915, William R. Slimmer lured customers into McCardell's Restaurant at 120 North Market Street by tempting them with one of the delicious homemade desserts. The desserts were the reason most people referred to the establishment as McCardell's Confectioners. The building burned several times over the years, the largest fire occurring shortly after this picture was taken. The current tenant of the building is the Frederick County Department of Social Services.

*Preparations are underway to begin construction of the post office building on Patrick Street in 1917. This spot is now the parking lot for the post office. The building across the street was the trolley barn and is now the* Frederick News-Post *building. A trolley can be seen to the right of the building on Carroll Street.*

*These homes, circa 1918, on the second block of West Patrick Street were torn down in the late 1970s to make way for the new courthouse. Shown from left to right they are: 104 - the Bantz property; 106 - James Walker property (at one time home of the Blue and Grey Beauty Salon); 108 - J. Davis Byerly residence; 110 - Thomas A. Chapline property (previously owned by George Markell); 112 - Francis Markell property; and, 114 - Goldsborough property.*

*Frederick's "finest" pose outside City Hall in 1914. Left to right (front row) John Blume-nouer, Thomas Filby, William Fraley, and Jacob Quinn; (second row) John Englebrecht, Chief George Hoffman, and Charles Hoffman; (back row) Adam Bruchey and John Henry Adams. On August 8, 1922, a man by the name of William A. Stultz shot and killed Officer Adams at the corner of West Fourth and Bentz streets. Mr. Stultz was convicted and hanged for his crime.*

# CARL BROWN

## Boyhood Memories Circa 1915

*Courtesy of Jonathan Summers*

Upon reaching an advanced age, life-long Frederick resident Carl Brown (now 89) decided to record his memories of his childhood in Frederick City. Like the amateur historian and diarist Jacob Englebrecht before him, Brown created a written photograph of the world as he knew it in the early part of the 19th century. While his personal memoir does not chronicle the major national and international events of the era, it does offer a glimpse of day-to-day life in Frederick, a simpler, perhaps easier way of life.

"I was a bat boy for the Frederick Blue Ridge team when Buck Ramsey was manager," writes Brown. "I was bat boy the year Frederick won the Junior World Series. When the winner of the Blue Ridge League, Frederick, played the winner of the Eastern Shore League, Frederick won the title from Princess Anne. I got two dollars and a new ball."

In his memoir, Brown writes of the changing topography and growth of the City of Frederick. He offers the explanations he was told as a child for some of Frederick's street names and play areas, and remembers recreational activities lost to time.

"In the winter we did a lot of sled riding. Lambright Alley and South Market Street were our favorite sledding places. I never knew anyone to get hurt or injured by traffic. We also did a lot of ice skating on Burger Pond off Broadway for five cents, which entitled you to skate all day. This was something you could do all day after day as the ice did not melt as fast as it does now."

Brown writes of early com-merce in Frederick.

"There are many ways that people earned income that are long gone. Benny, a black man, would come around several times a year to repair umbrellas. He carried a set of tools, staves for umbrellas, and cloth to repair any rip in the umbrella. He did a very good job for 15 to 25 cents. Mr. Curtis Geiser was one person who made his living making reed baskets. He collected the reed along the C&O Canal near Tuscarora. A Mr. Zeller from B&O Avenue earned part of his living by coming to your home and making sauerkraut. There was a Mr. Billy Hilton who made homemade pretzels. A large pretzel cost one cent and an extra large two or three cents."

Life in a simpler time meant entertainment in simpler forms. "The Great Frederick Fair was one of the big events of the year. More people were in Frederick that week than any other in the year. Local people would come from outlying districts in their horse-drawn wagons. During the Fair, Market Street between Saint and Patrick would be lined with carriages from the visitors to the Fair. On Saturday before the Fair, the Fakers would arrive. The balloon man was a favorite with the kids. One balloon seller carried a cornet and he would stop and play a song several times in a block. Then there were three Italians with accordions and they would play for your entertainment, then take up a collection."

*Courtesy of Jonathan Summers*

And if entertainment was simple, simpler still was education in the early 1900s.

"Elm Street School was for boys only, no girls in those days. We had Military Training at Elm Street School. There were three companies, A, B, C. We would drill every Friday and we had blue uniforms. In the last year at Elm Street the girls came and everything was different then."

Brown's memories recall incidents of life in Frederick that are lost to time.

"There were all kinds of bells in Frederick. The most notable were the church bells and the fire company bells. We all know what the church bells were used for. The fire company bells were rung to call members to fight fires. The bells were also rung when a member of the company died. This is not done anymore. When the courthouse bell was rung a Mr. Moberly would stand on the courthouse steps and cry, 'All ye, All ye, who have business with the circuit court of Frederick County, please draw nigh.' There was another bell I remember. It was a gong-type bell on the wall of the Market House. The market master used this bell when it was time to open for business."

Carl Brown, born in Frederick in 1906, is an amateur historian who offers information about Frederick in his role as part-time curator of the Maryland Room of C. Burr Artz Library in Frederick.

*South Carroll Street looking north, circa 1908. The Frederick County Farmers Exchange building was on the left, and the Mountain City Mill occupied the three-story building on the right.*

*This saloon and hotel on the corner of West All Saints and South Market streets, across from the B&O station, was owned by J.A. Kidwaller, circa 1920. The small shed on the building was used as a fish market.*

*The Buffalo Hotel and the New City Hotel, were two popular estab-
lishments located on the first block of West Patrick Street, circa 1916.*

*Employees of Haller Dry
Goods Store, circa 1920.
The establishment was
located at 17-19 North
Market Street until the
1940s. In addition to
yard goods, it carried
a full line of ladies'
ready-to-wear and mens'
furnishings. The gentle-
man in the back is John
Haller, who owned the
store with his brothers,
Tom and Edward.*

*In 1922, J. Paul Delphey (center) was so successful selling motorcycles that William Harley (left) and John Davidson (right) traveled to Frederick to meet him. They were photographed at the Patrick Street Bridge over Carroll Creek.*

*Before the advent of traffic lights, there were traffic policemen. In 1920, it was necessary to provide assistance with traffic control between horses and horsepower at the Square Corner.*

Courtesy of Paul and Rita Gordon

Courtesy of Julien P. Delphey

A view of Baker Park from College Avenue, circa 1925. At the time this photo was taken, West Second Street has not yet been extended past the Maryland National Guard Armory. The German Reformed Church graveyard (to the left of the armory) had recently been deeded to the city and is today the site of Memorial Park. The mill pond that flowed through a mill race to the Zentz Mill and then into Carroll Creek was located west of the cemetery. Mountain City Creamery was located between the armory and the mill. The large building to the right was the Francis Scott Key Hotel, now Homewood Retirement Center.

J. Paul Delphey (left)
and two friends
display their trophies.

*A group of members pose outside the Young Men's Christian Association (YMCA) on West Church Street, circa 1925. Left to right (front row) Dr. Harry C. Hull, James Etchison, Lincoln Engelbrecht, Paul Willard, William Schmidt, Clark Wizowski, Bernard Davis, Casper Cline, Jr., Jacob Ramsberg, Judge Robert E. Clapp, Jr.; (second row) Edward Miller, (unidentified), Stanley Staley, Bill Carter, Bill Roderick, Caroll James, Adrien L. McCardell, Jr.; (third row) Irving Thomas, Robert Miller, (unidentified), Jack Markey, Joseph H. Apple, Jr.; (fourth row) David Yinger, Louis L. Wilson, Alvin Quinn, Wm. K. Clingmen.*

*A circa 1926 aerial photo of the "Golden Mile" before it was "golden" (looking south from Shookstown Road). The road running at a slight angle across the top third of the photograph is Route 40. The road just to the left of center connected with Route 40 is Willowdale Drive. Above Route 40 to the right is the McCain Orchards, where the Hillcrest developement is now located. The Baker family home, Waverly Manor, can be seen to the left in the photograph, (now The Manor apartment complex) and a small stretch of Shookstown Road can be seen in the lower left-hand corner.*

*An aerial view of Frederick looking south, circa 1929. Market Street runs through the center of the photo. Many landmarks are easily recognized – Maryland School for the Deaf, Visitation Academy, the armory, North Market Street School, courthouse, B&O railroad yard, and all of the church spires.*

*Michael's Auto Tire Company on the corner of South Bentz and West Patrick streets, circa 1927, was razed to widen South Bentz Street.*

*West Patrick Street iron bridge over Carroll Creek , circa 1926. Keefer Brothers plumbing building was on the left, now the site of the re-constructed Barbara Fritchie house.*

*The iron bridge crossing over Carroll Creek on South Market Street in 1927. Note the bend in the trolley tracks.*

*Markell & Ford Coal and Wood on the east side of Carroll Creek in 1927. The coal yard was directly across from the building that is today the Delaplaine Visual Arts Center.*

*Wilcoxon & Brown Lumber Company on West Second and Bentz streets in November 1927. The building was later demolished and replaced with the Calvary United Methodist Church.*

*Looking north on South Market Street from the cupola of the United Fire Company in 1927.*

*The Zentz Mill on Bentz Street after it was destroyed by fire on June 24, 1926.*

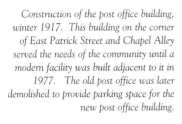

*The ticket office of the Pennsylvania Railroad in November 1927 was located on the corner of Church and East streets. The buildings pictured were removed in the 1930s for the expansion of the Everedy Company. The building on the far right is now the largest building in the Everedy Square complex and is the home of many businesses, including Tauraso's Ristorante and Frederick Magazine.*

*Construction of the post office building, winter 1917. This building on the corner of East Patrick Street and Chapel Alley served the needs of the community until a modern facility was built adjacent to it in 1977. The old post office was later demolished to provide parking space for the new post office building.*

*This view of Frederick looks northwest from above the B&O railroad yard, circa 1929. The spires are again prominent, as well as the post office, armory, and the area we now know as Baker Park.*

Courtesy of the Joseph Baker Family

Courtesy of Mrs. Nathan Jacobson

*Jacobson's Department Store, circa 1927, was one of the first full-service department stores in Frederick. It operated successfully from 1910 to the 1960s when Routzahn's purchased the property at 69 South Market Street for use as an outlet location.*

Courtesy of Carl Brown

*Central Garage was located on the southwest corner of West Patrick and Brewer's Alley. The building was razed to widen Brewer's Alley (now Court Street from Patrick to South streets), circa 1927.*

*A view of the Square Corner, looking east from the roof of the Francis Scott Key Hotel, circa 1920.*

*All of these buildings on Brewer's Alley, (now Court Street from Patrick to South streets) were razed to widen the street, circa 1927.*

*A view of Carroll Creek from College Parkway before the street was officially opened on April 8, 1928.*

*A view of high water in Carroll Creek taken from the South Market Street bridge looking east, June 19, 1928.*

*The law office of J.F. and E.L. Smith on the corner of West Second and North Court streets, circa 1929. The building was later removed to widen Court Street.*

*Looking north on North Bentz Street from the corner of West Fourth Street, circa 1928. The photo was taken prior to the removal of the cannon (lower right) to widen Fourth Street.*

Trinity Chapel viewed through the construction site of the the McCrory building on West Patrick Street in July 1928.

The city parking lot on Ice Street (now South Court Street) in February 1929.

This photo of the construction site of the Bentz Street bridge over Carroll Creek, June 1928, shows the stone foundation of the old swinging bridge prior to its removal.

*South Bentz Street looking north from the intersection of Bentz and West All Saints streets, circa 1928.*

Courtesy of Carl Brown

Courtesy of Carl Brown

*Looking northeast from Carroll Parkway (toward Baker Park) from the construction site of Parkway School in February, 1929.*

*North Bentz Street looking north from Patrick Street in 1928. The building with the Coca-Cola advertisement was demolished to widen the street.*

Courtesy of Carl Brown

Courtesy of Carl Brown

Junior Engine Company,
February 1929.

Courtesy of Carl Brown

Shops on South Market Street, circa 1928,
included P.L. Hargett's Hardware, Diamond
Bowling Alley, Buckey's Tobacco Shop, and
Angevine's.

A view of South
Jefferson Street
looking north in
April 1929. The
building to the right
of the Gulf station
was later torn down
to open North
Jefferson Street.

Courtesy of Carl Brown

A 1929 view of Frederick looking north from the tower of Calvary United Methodist Church.

Construction of Calvary United Methodist Church in December 1929. The church was built on the site of the Wilcoxon & Brown lumber yard on the corner of West Second and North Bentz streets.

This building, circa 1929, was the site of the Emergency Hospital on the corner of West South and South Market streets. The building was at one time a boardinghouse and later a soda fountain. The building was eventually razed, and the lot was the site of the parking lot for the downtown location of the Donald B. Rice Tire Company.

The "Johnny Swamper" firemen of United Fire Company bid farewell to the beloved "Lily of the Swamp," which was given to the Smithsonian Institution on February 23, 1933. From left to right are William Smith, Monroe Ryan, Thomas Chew, Fritchie Haure, Adam Bruchey, Marshall Stockman, Benton Knodle, and Richard Heck.

One of the Markell & Ford coal delivery trucks, circa 1930.

This photo of Memorial Park was taken from the bell tower of Calvary United Methodist Church in February 1930.

The armory and
Carroll Creek from
the bell tower of
Calvary United
Methodist Church
in February 1930.
In the distance is
Parkway School.
Note the absence of
automobile traffic.

*Courtesy of Carl Brown*

*Courtesy of Carl Brown*

During the severe drought that occurred in
October 1930, the "Lily of the Swamp" was
used to pump water. Standing on the wall
is Walter Lipps and next to the pumper is
Billy Ramsburg.

The A&P store on North Market Street, circa 1930. Originally
located on South Market Street (present site of Griff's restaurant),
it was moved to North Market Street across from City Hall in the
late 1930s and in the 1950s moved again to Court Street (present
site of the parking deck). The store manager, Orville Webster
Shinnick, is standing behind the counter on the left.

*Courtesy of Virginia Abrecht Joy*

Hershberger's Bakery and Restaurant,
circa 1930, at 213 North Market Street.
The business was owned and operated by
Webster Smith and managed by his son,
Cash Smith. Mr. Smith also owned the
Model Steam Bakery in Taneytown. Bread
was baked at Market Street, and cakes, pies,
and rolls were baked at their East Patrick
Street facility (now home of The Deli).
The bread and baked goods were delivered
throughout the county in the bakery's fleet
of delivery trucks.

In her will in 1887 Margaret Thomas Artz, the widow of Christian Burr Artz, left money to
build a library in her husband's memory. She required that of the three permanent board
members, one must be a member of the Evangelical Reformed Church and another a member
of All Saints Episcopal Church. The library was built on the site of Frederick College on
Record and Council streets in 1936. On March 29, 1982, the library moved to a larger,
more modern building located at 110 East Patrick Street.

Courtesy of Mrs. Betty Sulcer

Barties' Peanut Palace, "Home of Good Eats and Good Beer," circa 1937, was located at 53 South Market Street. The Palace was owned by Millard Ernest Barthlow (far right), shown here with son Russell Barthlow, Earl Orndorff, and Alvie Sulcer. The building is located along Carroll Creek.

Ebert's Ice Cream was built in 1931 on North Market Street. In addition to delicious ice cream treats, Ebert's served breakfast, lunch, and dinner until it closed in 1968. The building is now the site of Letterio's Italian Restaurant. This photo was taken at Christmas, 1931.

Authors' Collection

"Louie" parked his ice cream cart near Baker Park and sold ice cream cones for 10 cents to students after school. Enjoying ice cream cones in 1934 are, left to right: Helen Potts Bowman, Kitty Howard Gordon, Libby Fisher Richards, and Ann Powell Potts.

During the 1930s, many area residents participated in walk-athons. In 1932 Molly and Bob were the winners at a walkathon held in a large tent pitched on the property where Route 40 and Alternate 40 begin (now the site of Triangle Shell).

Blue Ridge Lines was Frederick's first bus service, started in the 1920s by W.C. Hann. Located on West Patrick Street, Potomac Edison bought the line in 1938, and Greyhound acquired it in 1955 and moved it to the present location on East All Saints Street. Photographed are the employees of the Union Manufacturing Co. boarding for their annual trip to Tolchester Beach, circa 1936.

*Frederick Municipal Putting Course, located near the intersection of Bentz Street and Carroll Parkway, circa June 1930, was replaced by the Tiny Tot playground in 1946.*

*The Frederick Theater on North Market Street, circa 1936. During the 1930s and 1940s this theater (now the site of Rogers Office Supply) entertained patrons by showing movies on the only "silvertone" screen in town.*

The Opera House, circa 1940. Built in 1872 and operated by the City of Frederick, the Opera House was located at 124 North Market Street. It changed hands many times over the years; its last owner was Dan Weinberg. The citizens of Frederick were entertained by many different types of performers, including musical reviews, animal acts, operas, and motion pictures. On Saturday afternoons the Opera House featured the most recent "cliffhanger," which guaranteed patrons would return the next week. The building served for many years as Frederick's City Hall.

An aerial view looking south of the northernmost part of North Market Street, circa 1940. The building in the lower right is Ebert's Dairy. The large group of buildings just above the center of the photo is the Odd Fellows Home.

*The Empire Theater on North Market Street, circa 1930, was located in the same building as Farmers and Mechanics National Bank. To the right is the Opera House.*

**"CHARLIE" KELLER**

**21. CHARLES ERNEST KELLER**

Outfielder    New York Yankees

Born: Middletown, Md.    September 12, 1916
Bats: Left    Throws: Right
Height: 5' 10"    Weight: 190 lbs.

Charlie Keller did not hit as often last year as he did in 1939 when he was the most sensational rookie in the American League, but he wielded a heavier bat for the New York Yankees. Keller fell to .286 against his .334 of the previous year but he drove in 93 runs, hit 21 homers and highlighted his season with three home runs in one game on July 28th. The University of Maryland grad looms as one of the strongest points in the Yankee campaign to regain their world laurels this year.

**PLAY BALL**
*Sports Hall of Fame*
Also ask for BLONY Super Bubble Gum, "the sweet that lasts longer."
© 1941    GUM, INC., Phila., Pa.

*The front and back of Charlie "King Kong" Keller's 1941 baseball card. Charles Ernest Keller, Jr., graduate of Middletown High School and the University of Maryland, was signed by the New York Yankees in 1937. In 13 years he hit 189 home runs and had a lifetime average of .286. As a Yankee, he played in the World Series in 1939, 1941, 1942, and 1943, with a .306 batting average. He was traded to Detroit and played there from 1950 - 1951, and in 1952 he ended his career with the Yankees. Charlie Keller died in Frederick on May 23, 1990, at the age of 73. His brother, Hall Keller, played for the Washington Senators from 1949 to 1952.*

# JOSEPH DILL BAKER

Joseph Dill Baker, the son of Daniel and Catherine Finger Baker, was born in Buckeystown April 2, 1854. At the age of 22 he was admitted to the firm of Daniel Baker & Sons. He moved to Frederick in 1877 and built Waverly Manor estates, where he resided until his death in 1938. Mr. Baker was a very successful businessman who went on to organize three banks: the Montgomery National Bank, Rockville, Md. (1883); Citizens National Bank, Frederick (1886); and the Peoples National Bank, Leesburg, Va. (1888). He served as the president of all three.

Joseph Dill Baker was a great philanthropist. At the age of 34, he refunded the bonded indebtedness of Frederick city. In 1898, with his brothers, William G. and Daniel, he founded the Buckingham School for the education of underprivileged boys. To ensure its continued support, he left upon his death one-fourth of his estate to the school. He donated the land for the building of the YMCA and gave generously to Hood College. Together with

*Authors' Collection*

*Authors' Collection*

Mrs. Baker, he built a new wing to the Home for the Aged, while greatly enlarging the endowment of the institution, and built the Baker Wing to the Frederick City Hospital, which provided hospitalization for black citizens. He made possible the public park, that bears his name, and also gave to the city Mullinix Park for use by the black community. In 1929, he purchased the Wilcoxon & Brown lumberyard property at the corner of Second and Bentz streets and donated the land and funds for the building of the Calvary United Methodist Church. He was well-liked and often took a personal interest in the people of the community, sharing their joys and sorrows and helping them out in time of trouble. In business, he willingly advised and assisted city officials whenever necessary, earning him the well-deserved title Frederick's "First Citizen."

The carillon bell tower in Baker Park was built in 1941 to his memorial at a cost of $45,000, which was quickly donated by the community. Designed by John B. Hamme of York, Pennsylvania, the tower is constructed of Baltimore County granite and stands 70 feet high. The original bells were made in Holland and are stationary; only the clappers move, weighing 15,000 pounds – the largest 3,500 pounds and the smallest 185 pounds. Each bell bears the inscription, "The Joseph Dill Baker Memorial." The largest bell reads, "This tower and carillon have been erected by his friends in loving memory of Joseph Dill Baker 1854 - 1938, whose life was benediction to this community, 1941." Nine new bells were purchased in 1966 bringing the total to 23 bells. A restoration project was completed in 1995 to recondition the bells and tower.

Frederick City Hall

# CHAPTER 7

## 1950-1995

Third Annual Tri-County Soap Box Derby Championship Held in Frederick

President Nixon Visits Fort Detrick to End Bio-Warfare Program

Carroll Creek Floods Downtown

Weinberg Center for the Performing Arts Established

New Court House Constructed

Start of Carroll Creek Flood Project

The Square Corner, looking west on West Patrick Street, in the summer of 1952. Although Market Street was one-way northbound as it is today, Patrick Street was still two-way. Two city police officers can be seen, believed to be Officer Murray (back to camera) and Officer "Chinky" Bell (on motorcycle at curb, partially obscured by car). The Western Maryland Trust Co. (now NationsBank) occupies the building on the corner, followed by Labell's, a woman's dress shop below Davis Studio. Farther up the street is the air-conditioned Tivoli Theater, showing a B western, entitled "Montana Territory," starring Tom McCallister, Wanda Hendrix, and Preston Foster. Next door was the Blue Ridge bus station, a liquor store, and the Buffalo Restaurant, one of Frederick's most popular seafood eateries. Across Ice (now South Court) Street was Leroy Hann's Amoco station and the Blue and Grey hair salon.

*Photo courtesy of M&B Printing*

In the 1950s the population of Frederick grew to nearly 24,000. By 1970 it had dropped to 23,641, due in large part to the closing of the U.S. Army's chemical and biological warfare facility at Fort Detrick. But a continuing influx of businesses into Frederick County and the construction of new housing developments in the city led to an increase in population through the '70s to approximately 30,000 in 1980.

The late '50s through the '60s and '70s saw some dramatic changes in Frederick. One of the most significant was the construction of Route 15 in the 1950s, which made Frederick easier to get both into and out of. The area's first shopping center, Frederick Shopping Center on West Seventh Street, opened in 1957, forever altering the way people did their shopping in Frederick. No longer was it necessary to go downtown to shop. When the two covered malls, Fredericktowne Mall on Route 40 and Francis Scott Key Mall on the south end of town came along in the 1970s, that change was complete—and nearly killed downtown retailers.

After suffering extensive damage in the devastating flood of 1976 when Carroll Creek overflowed its banks, downtown Frederick residents and business owners went to work

*The Square Corner at the intersection of Patrick and Market streets, circa 1952. Market Street was one-way, but traffic moved east and west on Patrick Street. The Patrick and Market street entrances to Cline's Furniture Store are located on either side of the Citizen's National Bank. Located to the left of Cline's are Colonial Music, Quynn's Hardware, and Remsberg's Jewelry.*

Courtesy of M&B Printing

*West Patrick Street looking east toward the bend, circa 1952. On the far left is a sign advertising the Barbara Fritchie house. Gem Laundry and Victory Cleaners were located on Patrick Street as well as the Frederick Motor Company and a Hertz rental car agency. A sign on the right indicates free parking is available for Delphey's sporting goods customers.*

to bring the town back to life. The downtown area was spruced up. All the power and telephone lines on Market Street were buried, trees were planted, the streets and sidewalks were repaired or replaced, and many downtown homes and businesses were restored. This rejuvenation helped reverse the outward migration from downtown that had begun in the late 1970s when shopping centers and suburbia began to pop up around the city. In the '80s, however, many new businesses and some of the finest restaurants in the region located downtown.

The town undertook one of its most ambitious projects ever in the 1980s with the start of the Carroll Creek Flood Control Project. Supporters said the massive and costly project would not only prevent another damaging flood, but also would result in a beautiful centerpiece for the city that would attract new life to downtown. Eventually, the creek is to be lined with park land and some new development. Progress slowed on the project during the country's economic recession in the late '80s, but continues today.

In recent years the City of Frederick has taken advantage of its lovely parks and has sponsored many activities there for (continued on page 233)

The Hotel Frederick, 327 North Market Street, circa 1952. The hotel and all but the last two buildings at the corner of North Market and West Fourth streets were torn down to make way for a parking lot at Carmack's grocery store. The restaurant at the left is now the home of the Olde Towne Tavern. The unsightly wires in this picture are now underground. Note the unique rooftop of Staub's (now Victorian Spirits) at 401 North Market Street.

The Barbara Fritchie Candy Factory and Restaurant, circa 1960. The buildings, located between routes 355 and 85 at Evergreen Point, are in use today as small retail outlets. In the early 1950s Price Electric built a clean room in part of the factory to allow them to manufacture relays.

# TRI-COUNTY SOAP BOX DERBY

On July 19, 1950, 33 boys competed in Frederick in the Third Annual Tri-County Soap Box Derby Championship. The winner would have the right to compete in the national championship in Akron, Ohio. The event was co-sponsored by the *Frederick News-Post*, Key Chevrolet Sales, and the Junior Chamber of Commerce.

Only children between the ages of 11 and 15 years of age could participate in the event. Each child had to design and build a motorless car within certain specifications, which were checked before the race. The weight of the car plus driver could not exceed 250 pounds. Each car had to be safe with good braking and steering systems, and could only be powered through the force of gravity.

Preceding the race was a parade that started at 1:25 p.m. from Derby Headquarters at 106 East Patrick Street. Wearing their Derby T-shirts and helmets, the 33 entrants, headed by Sheriff Guy Anders, marched in the procession.

The parade led to the site of the race, on West Patrick Street, a two-block stretch from Jefferson Street to Bentz Street. Approximately 3,500 persons lined both sides of the two-block course to watch the event.

Some of the officials for the race were starter Sam Maples, Jr., announcer Emmert Bowlus, and derby director Charles "Mac" Mathias. Others assisting in the event included cosponsors George B. Delaplaine, Jr., of the *News-Post* and Joseph P. Turner of Key Chevrolet Sales; former derby directors Dick Shoemaker and Mike Brittain; assistant director James McSherry; Walter G. Crowther, Jr.; Edward Etchison; and J.W. McDaniels.

Sitting in the judges' stand were cosponsors R. E. Delaplaine, W. T. Delaplaine, and John R. Cheatham, along with the mayors of Brunswick and Frederick, Stanley T. Virts and Elmer F. Munshower. Mayor Munshower awarded the prizes after the race was over.

The entrants were divided into two groups: 13- to 15-year-olds (Class A) and 11- to 12-year-olds (Class B). The derby was run in a series of heats, two cars racing at a time until Class A and Class B winners were determined.

The Class A and Class B winners competed for the Tri-County Derby Championship. The winner was 14-year old Basil Day, a Frederick High School ninth-grader, defeated Donald Tregoning. Basil was the cousin of the 1948 winner, Jimmy Burdette.

# FORT DETRICK

What we now know as Fort Detrick was once the site of the municipal airport. In 1929, the city government leased the 92-acre site to the United States government for use as a training camp. The first encampment of the 104th Aero Squadron, 29th Division of the Maryland National Guard, was held in August 1931, complete with DeHaviland O-38 observation biplanes. The squadron held its summer encampment at the field from 1931 to 1940. The facility was named in honor of the squadron's well-respected flight surgeon, Frederick-born Dr. Frederick Louis Detrick, who died in June 1931 at the age of 42.

During National Air Mail Week, the first mail was received and then dispatched from Detrick Field on May 19, 1939. Less than a week later, a B-24 bomber had engine trouble and was forced to make an emergency landing at the field. It landed nose up in a ditch near the trolley tracks on West Fourth Street, but suffered no serious damage and was able to take off the next day after refueling.

In the fall of 1940, Detrick Field was leased by joint agreement of the Maryland National Guard and the City of Frederick to the Civil Aeronautics Administration for use as a pilot training facility. The aircraft and pilots of the 104th Squadron and the cadets were assigned to anti-submarine patrols off the Atlantic coast in 1942. The last aircraft squadron at Detrick Field, the 2nd Bombardment Squadron, U.S. Army Air Corps, was consolidated at Brooklyn, New York's Military Terminal in September 1942, and was later deployed to England.

*The main entrance to Camp Detrick, on West Seventh Street, circa 1955. The facility became Fort Detrick in 1956.*

*Photos Courtesy of Fort Detrick*

In 1941, research into biological warfare began at Detrick under such strict secrecy that the citizens of Frederick were unaware of the activities in their midst until 1946. The facility became known as Camp Detrick on April 10, 1943, under the command of the United States Army Chemical Warfare Service, and was designated as a peacetime installation for biological research and development at the end of World War II. The research conducted at the facility consisted of the development of vaccines to defend against chemical and biological attacks, as well as the means to respond in the event of an attack by an enemy using biological weapons.

The facility was named Fort Detrick on February 1, 1956, when it became a permanent Army installation.

Fort Detrick now occupies about 1,200 acres, which are owned by the United States government. The main post is located in Area A, which consists of 800 acres. Water-and waste-treatment facilities are located along the banks of the Monocacy River. In 1946, the government purchased the 398-acre Krantz property along Shookstown Road for use as a test area and named it Area B.

On November 25, 1969, then-President Richard M. Nixon signed an executive order outlawing offensive biological research

*Construction of the "eight ball" at Camp Detrick, November 1947.*

In addition to cancer research, the facility also conducts research on infectious diseases, including AIDS. The development of medical equipment, and environmental quality and genetic engineering activities also take place at Fort Detrick. The facility includes a "maximum containment suite" capable of providing treatment to a patient while at the same time preventing further contamination.

The East Coast Telecommunications Center (ECTC), which has been located at Fort Detrick since 1959, is one of the key stations in the Defense Communications System. ECTC is responsible for the operation of a 250-line AUTODIN switching center and is one of 17 strategically located centers worldwide, relaying messages to and from the military, other government agencies, and NATO. In 1978, the Washington-Kremlin "hot line" was switched to satellite communications, and Fort Detrick's antennas were coupled with Soviet antennas via satellite to provide communications between the president of the United States and the Soviet premier.

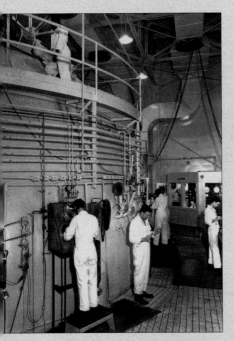

*An interior photo of the 40-foot-diameter, steel-plated test sphere known as the "eight ball" which was built at Camp Detrick in 1950 at a cost of $715,468. The 1-million-liter aerobiology chamber, the largest of its kind in the world, was used to test a variety of chemicals and dispersion apparatus. The sphere was not used after 1969, but was added to the National Register of Historic Places in 1977 for its contribution to science. The building surrounding the sphere burned to the ground in an electrical fire in 1974.*

in the United States, which many felt would cost the area jobs and have an adverse effect on the local economy. On October 19, 1971, President Nixon visited Fort Detrick, accompanied by Senator Charles McC. Mathias (R-MD), Senator J. Glenn Beall (D-MD), and Representative Goodloe E. Byron, Jr. (D-MD), as well as city, county, and Fort Detrick officials. The president announced that the former biological warfare complex would be used to fight cancer, America's number one enemy. The center is located on approximately 70 acres. Most of the 67 buildings in the complex have undergone extensive renovations. Approximately 2,000 people are employed here.

*President Richard M. Nixon exiting from Building 812, Army Headquarters, at Fort Detrick on October 19, 1971. The president is accompanied by (left to right) Congressman Goodloe Byron, Senator Charles McC. Mathias, and Senator J. Glenn Beall. Senator Mathias was largely responsible for the president retaining Detrick's unique research facility and converting it into the Frederick Cancer Research Facility.*

*An aerial photo of Fort Detrick looking northeast, circa 1961. The seven-story building in the center is Building 470, which was used to culture agents such as anthrax during the 1950s. The fields in the distance are now the heavily populated areas of Clover Hill, the developments beyond West Seventh Street, and Amber Meadows.*

*Scotty's Store was located at 300 North Market Street on the corner of East Third Street, circa 1952.*

*Clarke Place at South Market Street, February 1953. The building on the west side was razed in order to extend Madison Street to South Market.*

*West Seventh Street looking west toward Fairview Avenue before development, circa 1952, photographed from the grounds of the Elm Street School.*

*(continued from page 228)*

the citizens of Frederick. Among them are free concerts and theater during the summer months at the Baker Park bandshell. On Sunday mornings, anyone within hearing distance of the park's carillon is treated to lovely music. Every year thousands of Fredericktonians enjoy family festivities at the Fourth of July in Baker Park. In October the fall festival known as In the Street draws thousands to downtown Frederick.

Frederick is the site of many year-round athletic events: women's and men's slow-pitch softball, Little League and Babe Ruth baseball, soccer, lacrosse, and midget football. In August, the Frederick Open, sponsored by the Western Maryland Tennis Patrons, draws large crowds of spectators to watch some of the world-ranked players, as well as many of our local players, compete. In 1982, the 13-year-old team from Brooklyn, New York, won the first Babe Ruth World Series held at McCurdy Field in Frederick. In 1989, the Frederick Keys, Class A team of the Baltimore Orioles, took up residence in Frederick and played its first season at McCurdy Field. On April 19, 1990, Harry Grove Stadium officially opened as the home of the Frederick Keys, and each year the team breaks Carolina League attendance records.

*Courtesy of Carl Brown*

*This February 1953 photo shows the building, located at the corner of West South and Jefferson streets, which was demolished in order to extend South Street to West Patrick Street.*

*Judges and winners of the 1954 Easter parade. Judges (right to left, front row): Mayor Donald B. Rice, Ben Rosenour, Sonia Weiner (fourth from right), Stanley Weiner (directly behind). Winners of the best Easter egg basket were Richard Tuck and Judith Ann Tuck. The group photograph was taken in front of the City Opera House, which was featuring the movie "New Faces."*

*Courtesy of Frances Beall*

East Street looking north from Church Street, circa 1955. The shabby buildings in the picture were later renovated and contain the shops of what is now called Shab Row. The empty lot to the right was the site of a gas station and is now the home of Frederick Coffee Company.

Esso gas station on West Patrick Street along Carroll Creek in August 1955. To the left is the Dansburger Print shop on the northeast corner of Patrick and Bentz streets. A parking lot and a portion of the Carroll Creek project are now located in this area.

Located in a triangle with Baltimore (47 miles away) and Washington, D.C. (45 miles away), Frederick is a reasonable distance for commuters to travel to and from work. Many people feel that living in Frederick makes the drive worthwhile, as Frederick is surrounded by some of the most beautiful mountains in Maryland. It is a community steeped in tradition, proud of its heritage and accomplishments.

Frederick is a place of lively economic growth, balanced by some of the most popular and historic tourist attractions in the state. Our community owes its thanks to the generations of Frederick-tonians who have worked to preserve its historic sites and their history. ☆

*Courtesy of Carl Brown*

*Coffman Chapel under construction on the campus of Hood College, February 1954.*

*Courtesy of Carl Brown*

*The Dansburger Print Shop, located on the northeast corner of Bentz and West Patrick streets, August 1955. The building was later razed.*

*Local citizens along East Street watch as the Pennsylvania RR's last passenger train prepares to leave Frederick. The buildings behind the train are now home to Shab Row. The tall building to the rear is the Everedy Company, now Everedy Square.*

*Courtesy of Carl Brown*

Claire McCardell, American fashion designer, was born in Frederick on May 24, 1905. She attended Hood College from 1923 to 1925 and studied at the Parsons School of Fine and Applied Arts in New York and Paris from 1926 to 1928. McCardell was the foremost proponent of the "American Look," which emerged in fashion in the 1940s, designing comfortable, casually styled clothes that were also fashionable and made use of traditional American fabrics and details. Her designs included the famous denim Popover, or wrapped housedress, and the Monastic, a bias-cut dress with variable waistline. McCardell's repertoire was mass-manufactured by New Townley Frocks from 1942 until her death in 1958. That same year she was elected to the American Fashion Critics Hall of Fame. Her work often provides inspiration for clothing designers today.

The Blue Ridge Bus Terminal on West Patrick Street, July 1955. Considerable skill was required of the drivers to negotiate the buses into the narrow entrance. Part of the marquee of the Tivoli Theater, now the Weinberg Center, can be seen at the far left. Note the Potomac Edison logo above the sign. The building, along with several others, was eventually torn down and for many years a parking lot was located there. The space is now occupied by the Patrick Center.

*An aerial view of West Patrick Street showing the progress of construction of Route 15, circa 1956. The construction in the lower right of the photo is West Frederick Junior High School.*

*The Budweiser wagon, complete with a team of Clydesdales and a dalmatian, provides an interesting background for this photo of Carl Brown (left) taken on East Patrick Street in 1958. Note the box on the step in the lower left corner, which was used to keep home-delivered milk cold.*

A Pennsylvania R.R. train sits on the trestle prior to moving onto the B&O track in May 1960. Just visible behind the train is the Everedy Company.

*Courtesy of Carl Brown*

*Courtesy of Allen Routzahn*

*Courtesy of Paul and Rita Gordon*

A circa 1960 photo of the S.S. Kresge 5&10 Store located at 24 North Market Street

Allen Routzahn and store manager Tony Costantino in front of Routzahn's Budget Center on South Market Street, circa 1960.

A May 1961 photo, looking north on North Market Street, showing Farmers & Mechanics National Bank, City Hall, and the J.C. Penney Company.

*Courtesy of Carl Brown*

South Market Street looking north toward the Square Corner as it appeared in May 1961. The Kennedy Building, site of the Town House Bar & Grill, was razed to provide access to the municipal parking lot. The iron dog standing watch at the Federated Charities Building can be seen at the center of the photo.

*Courtesy of Carl Brown*

*Courtesy of Carl Brown*

East Patrick Street in 1964. The buildings in this picture were razed to build the current post office, dedicated in 1977. The building at the far right is the Everedy Company on East Street.

*Courtesy of Patsy Moore*

*Hendrickson's Department Store on North Market Street, circa 1970. John D. Hendrickson was born on the family farm in Baker's Valley in 1855. He attended the Frederick Academy and at the age of 16 began clerking at Parsons, a local dry goods store. He purchased the establishment in 1877 and five years later moved to 52 North Market Street. In 1887 he leased space in the newly completed Mutual Fire Insurance Company building at 42 North Market Street. Mr. Hendrickson served the community as a member of the building committee for the YMCA, and was a director of the Mount Olivet Cemetery Company and the Mutual Fire Insurance Company of Frederick County.*

*Courtesy of Carl Brown*

*Sears Roebuck, located on the south side of the first block of West Patrick Street, was the place to shop in 1963. "To Kill a Mockingbird" was playing at the Tivoli Theater.*

*Courtesy of Carl Brown*

*No longer standing, the once-prosperous Worman's Mill as it appeared in May 1963.*

*Courtesy of Carl Brown*

*West Patrick Street looking west around the bend in June 1963. Many of these buildings on the south side of the street were razed to make room for the Frederick County Courthouse.*

*Back and side view of the Krantz farmhouse (Schifferstadt) on Rosemont Avenue as seen from U.S. Route 15 in 1963. The barn to the left, in front of the farmhouse, is where the extended portion of West Second Street cuts through today to meet Rosemont.*

*Courtesy of Carl Brown*

*The first block of South Market Street looking north toward the Square Corner, circa 1963. Sam Miller's Store and the Albo Restaurant were later torn down to make room for a parking lot for Sears Roebuck. Beyond the restaurant are Landis Jewelry, Sears, King's Men's Wear, Western Maryland Trust Company (now NationsBank), and Frederick County National Bank.*

*A January 1963 view of South Wisner Street from East Patrick Street. Strucie's Grocery was later removed to widen Wisner Street.*

*The south side of the first block of West Patrick Street, looking east toward the Square Corner, May 1964. The Patrick Center is now located on the site once occupied by American Finance Company.*

Courtesy of Carl Brown

*North Market Street looking north from the Square Corner, May 1964. Frederick County National Bank has remodeled and expanded in recent years into the space once occupied by Gilbert's, Earl's Shoes, and Singer.*

Courtesy of Carl Brown

*The Francis Scott Key Hotel, circa 1964. Built in 1922 on the corner of West Patrick and North Court streets, it is now the Homewood Retirement Center.*

Courtesy of Carl Brown

North Market at Church Street looking north in 1964. The ground floor of the building at left (Rosenour Building) has been occupied by several dress shops and restaurants. Other establishments on this block were Shipley's Radio and TV and Bennett's.

*Courtesy of Carl Brown*

*Courtesy of Carl Brown*

An October 1963 view of Magnolia Avenue looking south toward Watkins Acres before the street was extended to West Second Street.

The north side of the second block of West Patrick Street in June 1964. The Hertz Rental Company was located in the Marken & Bielfeld Printing Building (third building from left), which was later torn down to make room for the expansion of the Ford Motor Company.

An October 1964 picture of the Markell & Ford Coal and Wood office located next to the bridge on Carroll Street. The building was later razed to make room for a parking lot for Key Chevrolet.

Civil War Centennial Parade, 1964. The home of Ralph Zimmerman (right), 208 East Patrick Street, was being razed to create a parking lot for the Eagles' Lodge.

*The north side of East Patrick Street looking toward the Square Corner in 1964. In the distance is the sign atop the Francis Scott Key Hotel. Although Routzahn's Department Store, Schroeder's Men's Wear, and Hiltner-Roelke have all closed, the Snow White Grill still operates in the same location.*

*The C&P Telephone Company building, August 1964. This building was razed so the company could build a larger telephone exchange.*

*Governor Thomas Johnson High School, located on North Market Street adjacent to Rose Hill Manor, opened in 1966.*

The city's electric light plant, located on the northeast corner of Second and East streets, January 1965.

The intersection of South Market and South streets, circa 1968. Businesses located along the left side of South Market Street included Rice's Tire Company (former site of the Emergency Hospital), Lough Monuments, Lyle's Barber Shop, and the Sandrette Beauty Shop. On the right were Thompson's Shoe Repair, Ogle's Market, and Null Auto Service and Radiator Repair.

*The former Groff mansion, located at the intersection of North Market and West Seventh streets, circa 1970. The building served as the home of radio station WFMD for many years. The building was razed in 1973, despite efforts to preserve it. A medical complex was to have been built on the site, but more than 20 years later, it's still a parking lot.*

*The new Frederick County Courthouse under construction on the corner of West Patrick and South Court streets, circa 1980. The bricks on the lower portion of the building to the right are all that remain of the facade of the John Hanson house, the front portion of which was to be incorporated into the courthouse complex. The rest of the Hanson building was removed.*

Routzahn's Department Store, on the
corner of North Market Street and East
Patrick Street, 1980.

Bert Anderson, standing in front of Everedy
Square, 1989. He acquired and restored the
old Frederick Trading Co. building located
at 125 East Street for his business, Antique
Imports, in 1973. In 1977, he acquired and
developed the adjacent row houses on East
Street, known as "Shab Row," into a retail
center. In 1984, he also purchased and
developed the old Everedy Company, which
earlier had been owned by the Lebherz
brothers, manufacturers of kitchen and
household products. Today, the Shab Row
and Everedy Square business complex holds
61 retail and office tenants.

# THE WEINBERG CENTER

The Weinberg Center for the Arts, located on the first block of West Patrick Street, has become an important part of the Frederick arts community, playing host to big-name music and comedy acts, national touring companies, as well as locally produced concerts, dance, opera, and theater. The Fredericktowne Players is its resident theater company. The theater seats 1,181 people and does more than 200 shows a year. The center was named for Dan and Alyce Weinberg, who along with their children, Aldan and Danyce, donated the building to the City of Frederick in the mid-1970s.

The building, however, has been known for most of its life as the Tivoli Theater, showing mostly first-run movies. The Tivoli, built in the tradition of the grand movie palaces, opened on December 23, 1926, when it presented "The Strong Man," a silent film accompanied by the theater's Mighty Wurlitzer pipe organ. The new theater, deco-

*A 1992 photo of the Weinberg Center taken from the stage shows the extensive restoration work at the theater.*

rated with massive chandeliers and velvet rocking chairs, cost $350,000 to build.

At that time the Tivoli's competition was the the Frederick Theater and the Opera House, all operating in a two-block area

*Courtesy of Scott Suchman*

*A balcony view of the Baltimore Symphony Orchestra during a performance at the Weinberg Center in 1994.*

downtown. The Frederick Theater specialized in westerns and was the most popular. The Opera House also showed some westerns, while the Tivoli was considered higher class, showing more romantic flicks.

In the 1930s, the Tivoli became Frederick's first public air-conditioned building. A local physician, Dr. Eddie Thomas, who was both a movie and horse-racing fan, is responsible for cooling the building. W. L. Brann, who had entered in California's prestigious Santa Anita handicap a horse named Challedon from his farm near Walkersville, had invited Dr. Thomas to go with him to attend the event. While in California, Thomas happened to meet Jack Warner of Warner

Authors' Collection

Brothers at a pre-race party. He told Warner to put his money on Challedon. Warner took the advice and collected a fortune in winnings.

Warner wanted to repay Thomas, and so Thomas, who never missed a show at the Tivoli, requested that Warner air condition the theater, which happened to be owned by Warner Brothers at the time. The two-ton compressors were built on site at a cost of $100,000. Thereafter, on warm days many patrons would come just to cool off.

In the 1960s and 1970s the Tivoli gradually lost its audiences to the newer, more modern multiplex theaters in the shopping malls. By the mid-1970s the grand old theater was showing mostly X-rated pictures.

Late on the night of October 8, 1976, the building was almost destroyed by the city's devastating flood. The storm-driven waters of Carroll Creek peaked three feet above the stage, submerging the velvet-covered

seats and floating the organ onto the stage.

The Tivoli building was donated to the city and restored through the hard work and generosity of the community, for a cost of $175,000. On February 9, 1978, it was officially opened as the Weinberg Center for the Arts.

*A 1992 photo of the carbon arc movie projectors that were used to show newsreels and movies at the Tivoli Theater for 50 years. The projectors are no longer operational, but are still located in the projection room at the Weinberg Center, which is currently being used as the office of the Weinberg's technical director.*

*The ticket booth of the Tivoli Theater at the main entrance on West Patrick Street.*

*A 1995 view of the marquee and entrance to the Weinberg Center for the Arts.*

*Darlene Wiles' classic photograph highlights the rescue effort that took place during the flood in October 1976. Susie (left) and Janet Hargett, along with Susie's horses and their puppy, were rescued on East Patrick Street by United firemen George Heffner and Franklin Blank.*

# CARROLL CREEK

On Saturday, October 9, 1976, Carroll Creek overflowed its banks and brought Frederick to a standstill. The rain began on September 30 and came down steadily for more than a week. By Saturday morning, more than seven inches of rain had fallen. It was pouring at 8:30 a.m., and water was beginning to spill over the banks of the creek. Local businesses were preparing to open, but by 10 a.m., the only way to travel on South Market Street was by boat. The flood waters did not begin to recede until about 2 p.m. Many basements flooded, and water stood knee deep in most buildings along the creek. All available firemen, policemen, and rescue

crews quickly mobilized, and with the assistance of many volunteers, began the evacuation of residents trapped in their homes. Due to the well-coordinated effort of all involved, no deaths occurred, and the injured were quickly located and treated. Shelter was provided by the Red Cross at the Maryland School for the Deaf. Most power, telephone, and water services were restored within 24 hours. At the urging of Mayor Ron Young and the intervention of Governor Marvin Mandel, President Gerald Ford declared the City of Frederick a disaster area. Disaster relief funds for flood victims amounted to $5.1 million, nowhere near the amount

*Looking north from above South Market Street on the morning of October 9, 1976.*

A view of the Carroll Creek flood control construction between Carroll Street and South Market Street in 1995.

required to cover the estimated $25 million in damages. Few homeowners or businesses had flood insurance. Many of the structures along the east side of South Market Street were so severely damaged that they were condemned. It took months for some businesses to re-open, and others closed their doors for good. Frederick's fire companies volunteered to pump water out of basements and help with the removal of mud. The city government, aided by many volunteers, responded immediately and began the time-consuming task of clearing the tons of mud from streets and buildings.

This was the fourth major flood to occur in the city. Although it had been almost 90 years since the last serious flood, the devastation of this flood caused citizens to demand that something be done to prevent such an event ever happening again.

Frederick is built on a flood plain. Prior to the flood, a plan was in the works to clean and widen Carroll Creek. In order to raise federal and state funds for the flood plan, it was necessary to show the potential for economic development. New federal regulations prohibit building on a flood plain. The

Frederick native Ronald N. Young, mayor of Frederick from 1974 through 1990, played a major role in the development of the Carroll Creek project.

*A recent view of construction along the creek looking west toward the Delaplaine Visual Arts Center on Carroll Street.*

$57.5-million Carroll Creek project will protect the city from flooding and is believed to be the economic salvation of downtown. The flood control plan calls for 1.3 miles of concrete conduit running from Baker Park to Highland Street. The conduit will follow the original creek bed and will control and convey floodwater to the Monocacy River. The conduit will also be used to contain backwater flooding of the Monocacy into the eastern part of Frederick. Upon completion of the flood control project, several parks are planned to enhance the creek property. The first, Market Place, will welcome citizens and visitors to downtown Frederick.

*A 1995 view of the original creek bed. The building at top left is the former site of the Frederick Seamless Hosiery Company, founded in 1887.*

*Looking east across South Market Street toward the parking deck on East Patrick Street. When the Carroll Creek project is completed, all areas along the creek will look similar to this.*

*Looking west from South Market Street. To the right is the Frederick County Courthouse and to the far right is the parking deck on Court Street.*

*The 1994 Frederick Festival of the Arts was the first major event to be held along Carroll Creek.*

*Skyview from the roof of the Patrick Center looking east toward the Square Corner and East Patrick Street, 1992.*

*Frederick County National Bank at the corner of West Patrick and North Market streets, December 1993. Note the new facade of the two adjacent buildings to the right of the bank, which were restored in 1992 to accommodate the bank's growth.*

*Frederick native Charles McC. Mathias represented Frederick in the House of Representatives from 1960-1968 and the United States Senate from 1968-1987. Senator Mathias was instrumental in Fort Detrick's conversion from biological warfare center to cancer research during the Nixon administration.*

A 1992 photo of a portion of the crowd enjoying the "In the Street" festivities. Originally organized to celebrate the completion of the the project to place all overhead wires underground, it has become an annual event attracting thousands of people.

A 1993 bird's-eye view of the Frederick County Courthouse.

A commemorative envelope issued and cancelled at Frederick for the centennial celebration of the Maryland State Firemen's Association held in Frederick in 1993.

# THE FREDERICK KEYS

In the spring of 1988, Baseball and Sports Associates, Inc. actively pursued and ultimately acquired the baseball franchise formerly located in Williamsport, Pennsylvania. After lengthy negotiations with the Baltimore Orioles, Carolina League officials, Eastern League officials, the National Association of Professional Baseball Leagues, the City of Frederick, and local youth baseball officials, an agreement was finally reached to allow Frederick to become the home of a Class A baseball team. Financing would come from city, county, and state funds. Mr. and Mrs. M. J. Grove donated $250,000 to be used toward the building of a new stadium to be named in honor of Mr. Grove's father, James Henry "Harry" Grove, who had been involved with the *Frederick Hustlers,* a member of the Blue Ridge League, until his

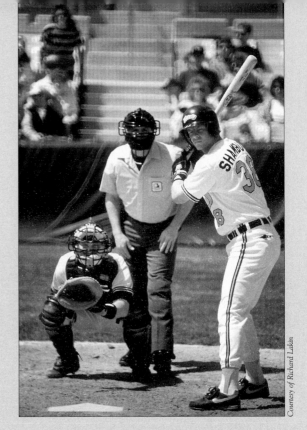

*Courtesy of Richard Lakin*

Frederick Keys designated hitter Ken Shamburg at the plate in 1990.

Frederick News-Post *photographer Sam Yu's photo of a full house at Harry Grove Stadium, September 5, 1994. Keys mascot Keyote (center) chats with young fans.*

Photo by Sam Yu, Courtesy of Frederick Keys

death in 1930.

The Frederick Keys, the Carolina League Class A affiliate of the Baltimore Orioles, played its first game at McCurdy Field on April 11, 1989, defeating the Kinston Indians.

The Keys were victorious when Harry Grove Stadium was officially opened on April 19, 1990. They defeated the Peninsula Pilots 5-4 in 11 innings. With attendance during the regular season at 277,802, the team went on to win the 1990 Carolina League Championship.

In 1991, seating was increased from 4,500 to 5,200. Twelve skyboxes and a restaurant/clubhouse were added. On June 8, 1991, President George Bush joined Mr. Grove in a box to watch the Keys play the Durham Bulls. Attendance in 1991 was 318,354.

Attendance continued to increase and in 1992, 329,592 fans, including President and Mrs. Bush and several of their grandchildren, cheered for the Keys. The single game attendance record was set in 1992, when 8,501 fans helped celebrate the 175th anniversary of Farmers & Mechanics Bank

with a fireworks display.

Attendance during the 1993 season was 351,146. In 1994, attendance was only 344,563, but it was still high enough that the team recorded its fifth consecutive season with the highest attendance in the Carolina League.

Several members of the Frederick Keys have gone on to play in the major leagues, including Arthur Rhodes, Anthony Telford, and David Segui. Brady Anderson, Mike Devereaux, and Billy Ripken have also played with the Keys while recovering from injuries. The player who brought the most attention to the Frederick Keys was first-round draft pick Ben McDonald. McDonald finally signed with the Orioles and made his professional pitching debut at McCurdy Field on August 23, 1989, against the Winston-Salem Spirits. Fans from all over the country saw McDonald pitch three innings and witnessed the Keys' first triple play in a 6-4 win. McDonald took the mound one more time that season. On August 27, against Durham, he struck out eight in five scoreless innings.

## '89 FREDERICK KEYS

**TOP ROW (left to right):** Mark Zeigler, assistant general manager; Keith Lupton, general manager; Andres Constant, David Segui, Luis Mercedes, Louie Paulino, Oneri Fleita, Francisco de la Rosa, Mike Deutsch, Jack Voigt, Scott Meadows, Anthony Telford, Dave Miller, Hector Bautista, Matt Hicks, radio announcer; Jim Halloran, director of group sales. **MIDDLE ROW:** Mike Linskey, Mike Cavers, Steve Mondile, Stacy Jones, Mike Pazik, pitching coach; Jerry Narron, manager; Doug Merrifield, trainer; Minnie Mendoza, Orioles roving instructor; Chris Myers, Mike Lehman. **FRONT ROW:** Roy Gilbert, Paris Hayden, Dan Simonds, Tom Harms, Ricky Gutierrez, Rodney Lofton, Stacey Burdick, Jason Bartee, bat boy. **NOT PICTURED:** Pete Palermo, Pete Rose II, Bob Williams, Larry Mims, Del Ahalt, Brent Bell, Arthur Rhodes, Jaime Pena, Doug Robbins, Mike Borgatti, Ken Shamburg, Zachary Kerr, David Riddle, Mark Bowden, Debbie Dickman, office manager.

*President George Bush and M. J. Grove chat during a game between the Frederick Keys and the Durham Bulls on June 8, 1991.*

A 1995 photo of Frederick's City Hall, formerly the Frederick County Courthouse.

The Delaplaine Visual Arts Center, 1994. Housed in the old Mountain City Mill on Carroll Street, the art gallery moved into the site after completing extensive restoration to the building in 1993. The new Carroll Street bridge is the site of the "Shared Vision" murals.

Authors' Collection

Paul Gordon poses on the steps of Frederick City Hall, 1989. Mr. Gordon served as mayor from 1990-1994.

The William Donald Schaefer Government Services Building under construction on Carroll Street will provide many new jobs for area residents. The building behind the office building was originally a mill, built in 1917 by Detrick and Gamble. The mill was connected to the warehouse (built in 1780) by a walkway. The mill building is being remodeled as Carroll Street Mercantile Antiques, and the walkway will soon be removed.

# PAINTING THE TOWN

Artist William Cochran proposed a series of murals in downtown Frederick in 1987 and initially met opposition from residents who could not envision the concept. Today, the murals are hallmarks of the downtown area. The first in the "Angels in the Architecture" series of murals, "Egress," painted in 1988 with artist Colleen Clapp, depicts wildfowl flying from an open window. It is painted on the corner of East Second and North Market streets. Second in the planned seven-part series is "Earthbound," painted with Paul Wilson on Church Street, depicting a pheasant and an elderly angel. The third completed painting, entitled "The Edge of Gravity," is located on the side of the Chamber of Commerce building on North Market Street. Putting work aside on the mural series, Cochran is at work on the Community Bridge mural project sponsored by Shared Vision. Located on the wing walls of the Carroll Street bridge—a part of the Carroll Creek project—the trompe l'oeil murals will transform the modern structure into an old stone bridge with ivy and details such as an iron gate and classical sculpture.

"The Edge of Gravity" painted by William Cochran on the Chamber of Commerce building. Frederick County received the first national charter issued by the U.S. Chamber of Commerce, May 21, 1912.

Muralist William Cochran and the trompe l'oeil version of the "Woman of Samaria" sculpture by William Henry Rinehart, painted on the Carroll Street bridge.

Authors' Collection

The mural, "Egress," is painted on this building, now Nicole's Delicatessen, at the corner of East Second and North Market streets. The building has been the site of several restaurants and grocery shops, most notably Cappello's Food Market.

"Earthbound," painted by William Cochran and Paul Wilson, appears on the Examiner building at the corner of North Market and Church streets, which houses the Orchard Restaurant.

*A 1995 view of Citizen's Truck Company (center) on Court Street, dwarfed by the Frederick County Courthouse and the parking deck.*

*The Patrick Center, adjacent to the parking deck, on the corner of South Court Street and West Patrick Street. The clock tower at right stands in front of the Frederick County Courthouse.*

*A 1995 photograph of the Fine Arts and Student Center, one of the many new buildings added to the Opossumtown Pike campus of Frederick Community College. The college began operating in 1957 when it offered evening classes conducted at Frederick High School. In 1966, the college moved to the North Market Street School building until the campus on Opossumtown Pike was dedicated on May 2, 1971.*

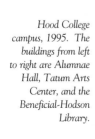

*Hood College campus, 1995. The buildings from left to right are Alumnae Hall, Tatum Arts Center, and the Beneficial-Hodson Library.*

*A view of Frederick's most famous landmark, the Clustered Spires, taken from Prospect Hall, 1994.*

Courtesy of Edwin Remsberg

# BIBLIOGRAPHY

Bevan, Thomas R. *220 Years...A History of the Catholic Community of the Frederick Valley.* Frederick: Catholic History, 1977.

*The Citizen: Historical and Industrial Edition* (newspaper). Frederick: October 28, 1904, Vol. 84, No. 15.

Delaplaine, Edward S. *Maryland in Law and History.* New York: Vantage Press, 1964.

Gordon, Paul P., and Rita S. Gordon. *A Playground of the Civil War.* Frederick: Paul and Rita Gordon, 1994.

Gordon, Paul P., and Rita S. Gordon. *A Textbook History of Frederick County.* Frederick: Board of Eduction of Frederick County, 1975.

Harwood, Herbert H. Jr. *Blue Ridge Trolley.* San Marino, California: Golden West Books, 1970.

Holdcraft, Jacob. *Names in Stone.* Two Volumes. Ann Arbor, Michigan, 1966.

Holt, John R. *Historic Frederick.* Frederick, 1949.

Markell, C. Sue. *Short Stories of Life in Frederick in 1830.* Frederick Attic Treasures, 1948.

Newhall, Beaumont. *The Daguerreotype in America.* New York: Dover Publications, Inc., 1976.

Newman, Parsons. *Three Historical Sketches of Frederick County.* Frederick: Historical Society of Frederick County, Inc., 1974.

Quynn, W. R. *Bicentennial History of Frederick City and County, Maryland.* Frederick: Bicentennial Committee of Frederick Chamber of Commerce, 1975.

Rice, Millard Milburn. *New Facts and Old Families: From the Records of Frederick County, Maryland.* California: The Monocacy Book Company, 1976.

Whitmore, Nancy F., and Timothy L. Cannon. *Frederick: A Pictorial History.* Frederick: Frederick County Landmarks Foundation, 1988.

Williams, T. J. C. *History of Frederick County, Maryland.* Frederick: Titsworth & Co., 1910; reprinted by Regional Publishing Co., Baltimore, 1979.

# AUTHORS' BIOGRAPHIES

Nancy F. Whitmore, a native of Massachusetts, is a graduate of the Chandler School for Women, Boston. She has resided in Frederick since 1966 with her husband, Mark. They have two sons, a daughter, and one granddaughter. She is manager of the Waldenbooks store in the FSK Mall. She is the co-author of two other books: *Ghosts and Legends of Frederick County* and *Frederick: A Pictorial History.*

Timothy L. Cannon, a native of Frederick, earned a bachelor's degree in mathematics from the University of Maryland and a master's degree in computer and information sciences from Hood College. He has worked in the computer field since 1978 and currently serves as a computer specialist at the U.S. Army Medical Research Institute of Infectious Diseases, located at Fort Detrick. He is the co-author of two other books: *Ghosts and Legends of Frederick County* and *Frederick: A Pictorial History.*

Tom Gorsline, a native of Michigan, earned a bachelor's degree in secondary education from Central Michigan University. He taught photojournalism and history for five years in the Michigan public school system. He founded Diversions Publications, Inc., in 1985 and publishes the monthly *Frederick Magazine* and the annual *Frederick County Newcomers/Visitors Guide.* He is also co-owner of OakLeaf Communications, Ltd., a Frederick-based design and marketing company. An avid photographer and darkroom enthusiast, he enjoys working with historic glass-plate negatives.

# M&B PRINTING
## 1885-1995

123 W. PATRICK ST.

*I*t all began in 1885, when Victor Marken & Jonathon Bielfeld bought their first hand-fed Colt Armory printing press along with a new Ryan foundry type and set up shop on the third floor of the old Citizens Bank. "Quality first" was Marken & Bielfeld's guiding principle from the start and within a few years the firm was well-known for fine printing at affordable prices. In 1904 the business was well-established and moved to three floors at 123-125 West Patrick Street, producing for many years under government contract the "Postmaster's Report" books used by every post office in the country.

In 1926 the firm incorporated and began producing brochures, booklets and post cards for the travel industry, which was then in its infancy. Successive years saw continued growth and in 1948, the company acquired the present facilities at West Seventh Street and Military Road. Several years later the company became one of the first local printers to enter the "offset-lithography" printing field.

Celebrating with considerable fanfare its 100th anniversary in 1985, Marken & Bielfeld, Inc. changed its name to M&B Printing, Inc. Continuing the print excellence standard set by Marken & Beilfeld, M&B has accumulated numerous awards over the years. In 1993, M&B became the newest member of the Corporate Press family, based in Landover, Maryland.

M&B Printing is proud to have made many contributions to our community over the years and has worked diligently to be a good corporate citizen since our founding. We salute the City of Frederick on its 250th Anniversary ... A superb location to live and work!

## *Another Proud Partner in Frederick's History*

1704 W. Seventh Street
Frederick, Maryland 21702
(301) 662-1195 or (800) 321-3545
Fax (301) 662-1228 or (800) 321-2829

***Among so many... We stand out!***